# A HISTORY OF BRITISH PADDLE STEAMERS

ANDREW GLADWELL

Ian Allan PUBLISHING

First published 2014

ISBN 978 0 7110 3742 7

Published by Ian Allan Publishing Ltd, Hersham, Surrey KT12 4RG.

Printed in Bulgaria.

Visit the Ian Allan Publishing website at *www.ianallanpublishing.com*

**FRONT COVER** Paddle steamers such as the *Princess Elizabeth* were a familiar sight around the piers and coastline of the UK, becoming an iconic part of the seaside for generations of holidaymakers. *Photo: Andrew Gladwell Collection*

**BACK COVER** *Waverley* is now the last sea-going paddle steamer in the world and carries on the tradition of travelling by paddle steamer that started over 200 years ago. *Andrew Gladwell*

**HALF TITLE PAGE** Officers of Cosen's *Majestic*. It shows Captain Philip St Barbe Rawle (right). He became master of the *Majestic* in 1901. He remained as senior master and Commodore of the Cosens fleet until his death in 1916. *PSPS Collection*

# Contents

Introduction                                                4

1   How it All Began and Early Years                        8

2   The Heyday of the Paddle Steamer                        24

3   Ferries and Paddle Steamers in Rivers and Estuaries     60

4   Life Aboard the Steamers                                76

5   Paddle Steamers at War                                  86

6   Postwar Decline                                         96

7   Years of Restoration and Preservation                   128

    Bibliography and Acknowledgements                       160

# Introduction

ABOVE *Waverley* approaching Clevedon in 2005. By this time, *Waverley* had been through her 'Heritage Rebuild' to preserve her for the future as well as to return her to her pristine 1947 condition. *Waverley, Kingswear Castle* and *Balmoral* are now the last pleasure vessels to cruise around the coastline of the UK. *Andrew Gladwell*

The sight of a paddle steamer visiting a seaside pier or cruising along the coastline is one of the most evocative images of the British seaside. These distinctive, colourful and hardworking little ships were full of character and had a happy seaside role. They became synonymous with the British institution of the seaside during their heyday as they plied between towns, piers and harbours giving pleasure and performing an important task. Paddle steamers, like steam locomotives, ocean liners and early motor cars, always conjure up an image of idyllic summer days when travel was a pleasure and not a chore. They also provided a comfortable and affordable means of travel and led to the development of the British seaside resort. They became key players in helping to develop the concept of holidays and leisure travel in the UK.

The Victorian era was a time when every product of the age had its own unique style. Architecture, consumer products, decorative arts and transport all developed to embrace new technology and materials to produce something that had not only evolved to perform a task but to look good as well. The paddle steamer was no exception and soon the typical steamer developed to show its distinctive features such as the paddle box, hissing engine and luxurious passenger accommodation.

The paddle steamer reacted to the changing needs of the population of the UK during the Victorian era resulting from the growth of urban living and the need to move more easily. With romantic, historic and evocative names, paddle steamers reflected the places at which they called. The sight of a colourful livery on the horizon heralded the start of a holiday and senses were aroused as the pleasure steamer transported adults and children to places far removed from everyday life.

**ABOVE** *Waverley* on the Firth of Clyde in the days before she was withdrawn in the early 1970s. Paddle steamers usually had names of local places or famous people. *Waverley's* name came from one of Sir Walter Scott's novels. *Andrew Gladwell*

**ABOVE** A Belle steamer prepares to arrive at Clacton Pier around 1905. Piers at seaside resorts such as Southend and Clacton developed large and important pier head facilities with refreshment rooms, shops, bandstands and rest rooms to cope with large numbers of passengers arriving and departing on paddle steamers. *Andrew Gladwell Collection*

**ABOVE** The *Columba* was one of the largest and most magnificent paddle steamers ever built. She was MacBrayne's flagship from 1879 until 1935 and operated on the first part of the 'Royal Route' to Ardrishaig for almost six decades. *Ron Jones Collection*

Paddle steamer fleets were also early examples of marketing, as each operating company had its own distinct livery that was applied to each steamer in the fleet. Brand loyalty was encouraged and each company did its best to ensure that its steamers looked better, had finer accommodation and gave a better experience than their competitors.

The heyday of the paddle and pleasure steamer was relatively short. Times of great profit and success were matched with periods of failure. This resulted in amalgamations between companies and routes. The lives of the steamers were often as spectacular as the scenery that was passed on a cruise. The story of the paddle steamer was one of constant change and adaptation to react to changing needs and tastes. Paddle steamers evolved to mirror the wider changes in the life of the UK and its seaside resorts.

Competition from rival operators did, though, have beneficial effects for most fleets. The heyday of the paddle steamer was typified by the introduction of larger steamers. Steamers were also introduced from other areas around the UK to obliterate rivals. Recycling was common and smaller displaced steamers were sold for service elsewhere where their size was better suited. The late Victorian and Edwardian heyday resulted in spectacular vessels that were great statements of speed and luxury, reflecting the great confidence of their proprietors. Throughout its rise and fall, the paddle steamer changed little in its design and many steamers experienced long lives of over 60 years. This was due in many ways to the fact that they were great survivors – by only operating for a few months of the year, they lasted for a long time. Their design and technology were excellent and little could be done to improve what was a fit-for-purpose product.

By the 1920s and 1930s things were starting to change. These changes reflected developments in technology as well as wider changes in leisure habits and transport. The years following World War 2 saw the position and fortune of the pleasure steamer change dramatically. Soon, the trickle of change became a deluge and the 1950s and 1960s witnessed a quick and spectacular end for steamers that had given pleasure

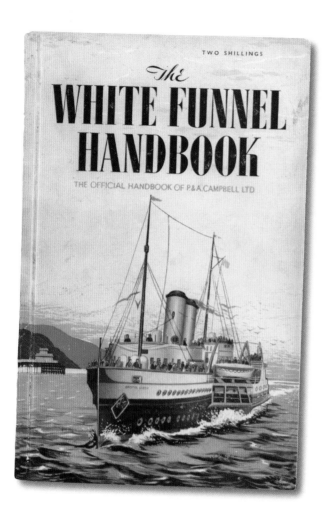

**ABOVE** A White Funnel guide from the 1950s. Each major operator produced a guide that was sold around the decks for a few pennies. It included maps, a guide to sights during the cruise, advertisements for seaside attractions at resorts and future cruise options.
*PSPS Collection*

**ABOVE** Handbill advertising cruises by the *Medway Queen* from Southend in 1962. *Medway Queen's* withdrawal in 1963 provoked a national campaign to save her. The campaign was a success and she was reprieved. Despite suffering an uncertain future at times thereafter, a hull rebuild was completed at Bristol in 2013.
*Andrew Gladwell Collection*

over many decades. It was a time when, all of a sudden, the previously aged but adequately working steamers were becoming uneconomic. With little or no potential to carry out necessary work, the inevitable was faced with placid acceptance and the steamers were withdrawn, their place taken by the flexibility and reliability of the motor car and cheap air travel. With the rise of interest in heritage, the pleasure steamer was able to survive through the 1960s but by this time the number of working examples could be counted on one hand. The years that followed experienced a revival where a leaner, more versatile fleet evolved, enabling the final few examples to be preserved and operated. New generations are still able to experience these pleasure steamers and to see them as nostalgic and totally different from the mundane and soulless motor car and motorway. Pleasure steamers have survived and today give pleasure to countless people around the UK as much as they did over a hundred years ago.

# 1

# How It All Began and Early Years

**ABOVE** The General Steam Navigation Company was formed in 1824 and provided popular paddle steamer services until it ceased operating in the mid-1960s. It became the most famous operator of paddle steamers on the River Thames. The last paddle steamer built for the GSNC for River Thames service was the *Royal Eagle*. *Andrew Gladwell*

8

The idea of moving a ship by revolving wheels with paddles placed at the side of the hull can be traced back to Roman times when the first paddle wheels were described. The principle of a paddle-propelled vessel continued to be discussed over following centuries, but a reliable vessel could never be developed due to the lack of an efficient and reliable means of propelling the vessel consistently over long distances. Paddle-propelled boats could never compete with the performance and predominance of sail-powered vessels at the time as the technology was not available to summon up enough power to turn wheels large enough to power a large ship. The reliance on wood in ship construction also meant that it was not possible to build a wheel that was strong enough to cope with large items of floating debris that often got entangled with the paddle wheel.

The Industrial Revolution produced advances in iron and steel manufacture as well as the development of steam power by pioneers such as Matthew Boulton and James Watt. This meant that the time had come for the paddle steamer to be developed to a point where it would become a serious means of propelling a ship. With these advances in technology and manufacture, came the commercial catalyst for large-scale change that would encompass trade, commerce and leisure.

In 1802, on the Forth & Clyde Canal in Scotland, William Symington designed the first paddle steam ship. The idea was slow to take off and it was to be another decade before the first commercially viable paddle steamer was fully developed on the Clyde. The wooden-hulled *Comet* entered service on 6 August 1812 and became the first paddle steamer to regularly operate with passengers in Europe. *Comet* was a truly revolutionary ship and became the catalyst that kick-started the development and adoption of the paddle steamer throughout the rivers and estuaries of the UK. *Comet* was quite small, measuring just 40ft in length by 10ft in width, and was built by John Wood of Port Glasgow with an engine manufactured by John Robertson of Glasgow. She covered her maiden voyage from Port Glasgow to Glasgow in three and a half hours. *Comet* immediately fired the enthusiasm of passengers who could now travel faster and in more comfort than in the past. The

**ABOVE** The first commercial paddle steamer was designed by Henry Bell and named *Comet*. Her arrival was not greeted universally with praise and many feared the 'spluttery' thing. However, her success meant that rival paddle steamers soon provided services to Firth of Clyde locations such as Largs, Rothesay, Inveraray and Campbeltown. *Andrew Gladwell Collection*

**LEFT** The Industrial Revolution brought about a number of important social and technological changes that provided the catalyst for the first commercial paddle steamer, the *Comet*, to enter service on the Clyde in 1812. Her importance was marked by anniversaries in 1912, 1962 and 2012. This mug was produced to mark her 150th anniversary in 1962. *PSPS Collection*

newly introduced paddle steamer was able to give people the ability to travel and for many this was a new concept. These revolutionary paddle steamers soon expanded their services to call at remote Firth of Clyde locations such as Campbeltown and Largs. They also opened up regular services on inland lochs such as Loch Lomond. The initial response from the public to these new paddle steamers was sometimes one of uncertainty as the energy and noise of steam replaced the peaceful and silent sail transport of the past. It was indeed a revolution in transport and, despite the inevitable apprehension of some it was soon embraced as the transport of the future.

When *Comet* made her debut on the River Clyde in 1812, nobody could have predicted the speed of change elsewhere

**RIGHT** *Comet* was a revolutionary vessel and transformed steam-propelled ships all over the UK but this model shows her simple layout. The fare for her was four shillings for the best cabin, and three shillings for the other cabin. Her stern cabin just had a table and seats for passengers. *Andrew Gladwell Collection*

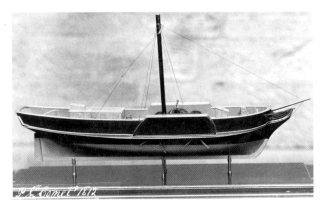

Princes Pier, Greenock

Barton Aqueduct and Bridge.    Nuttall, Church St., Eccles.

**ABOVE** Paddle steamers were a common sight at all of the great ports around the UK from the start of Queen Victoria's reign. They ferried goods as well as passengers. The *Ivanhoe* is seen here at the Barton Aqueduct on the Manchester Ship Canal that linked Manchester with the River Mersey. *Ron Jones Collection*

**LEFT** The Clyde provided an ideal location for paddle steamer services to develop. It possessed unrivalled shipbuilding skills at Glasgow and there was also a ready market for services which soon developed from the city to places such as Greenock and further afield on the Firth of Clyde. *Ron Jones*

THE COMET CENTENARY, 1812-1912.

MACNEUR & BRYDEN, HELENSBURGH.

**ABOVE** *Comet* became the first commercially viable paddle steamer in the UK when she entered service. Within little more than a decade, paddle steamers were to be seen all over the country. *Comet* was soon outclassed by newer and more advanced paddle steamers. She later operated at Oban but was shipwrecked in December 1820 at Craignish. *PSPS Collection*

**BELOW** The early paddle steamer *Industry* alongside the Broomielaw at Glasgow. Built in 1814, she was one of the earliest paddle steamers. She was constructed from oak from the Kilbirnie estate and had a folding funnel. She had a distinctive grinding sound which earned her the nickname of the 'Coffee Mill'. *Andrew Gladwell Collection*

ABOVE Paddle steamers enabled places to be linked easily without the need for bridges and tunnels to be constructed. Their shallow draft also ensured that they were able to reach most locations. A steamer is shown here at the mouth of the River Yealm.
*John Gilmore Collection*

ABOVE Resorts such as Rothesay grew significantly when the paddle steamer arrived. Very quickly, the steamers started new traditions of spending longer days at the seaside. The pier at Rothesay was one of the largest and busiest in the UK and was always a hive of activity. *PSPS Collection*

ABOVE People soon grasped the potential offered by the paddle steamer and leisure travel quickly developed. Huge queues were often to be seen lining piers and harbours to board the steamers. It was an age where people were travelling more than ever before and were no longer tied to their town or village. *Andrew Gladwell Collection*

ABOVE Llandudno Pier has dominated the North Wales resort since the town developed in Victorian times. Resorts such as Llandudno quickly embraced the paddle steamer. Services soon developed to create a boom in tourism. *Andrew Gladwell Collection*

around the UK. A little over two years later, the first paddle steamer went into service from London along the River Thames. The novel and now successful *Comet* was soon replicated at other major ports, towns and cities around the UK. The development and adoption of the paddle steamer came at the time when the Industrial Revolution was gathering massive momentum. The great cities of the industrial age needed ports and rivers to handle the vast increase in raw materials required to feed the mills and factories. The ports and rivers would in turn need steamers to transport the finished goods to their final destination. The paddle steamer, with its shallow draught and excellent manoeuvrability, could work in most ports. It was therefore well-suited to just about every location. Additionally, the paddle steamer provided the means to ferry workers easily and economically to their workplace from their homes in the new industrial cities and towns. Finally, these new

paddle steamers enabled people to travel for leisure more widely and affordably than ever before.

Despite initial shock at the new and noisy steam-propelled ship on the Clyde, people quickly embraced the paddle steamer when they realised the potential that it had to transform their lives. Transport revolutions on land required massive investment and large-scale geographic challenges had to be overcome to construct new canals, roads and railways. The paddle steamer was altogether a much more attractive and achievable option as it just needed water to operate on. It provided a particularly good way of joining up remote islands with small towns and villages with poor road links. These new paddle steamers also enabled people to travel more conveniently, quickly and cheaply than ever before. At the time, people rarely left their village or town. The arrival of the paddle steamer, although not widening the travel horizons of everybody

**ABOVE** Most areas of the UK experienced fierce competition between rival operators during Victorian times. The lucrative daytripper trade from seaside resorts such as Brighton was an obvious magnet for companies wanting to gain profit from holidaymakers. Fights and tearing down of posters often occurred between rival operators. *Andrew Gladwell Collection*

**ABOVE** A Belle Steamer alongside the pier next to London Bridge in front of St Magnus the Martyr Church. You can appreciate the problems of positioning a paddle steamer in this view, with the stern under part of the bridge. London was a great hub for paddle steamer services and many paddle steamers operated from the Pool of London. *Andrew Gladwell Collection*

**ABOVE** By the 1880s, the design and atmosphere of the typical paddle steamer had evolved. Steamers such as the *Galatea* of 1889 on the Firth of Clyde provided excellent passenger accommodation. Many paddle steamers were like mini liners with the range and quality of passenger accommodation that they offered. *PSPS Collection*

**ABOVE** *Ivanhoe* cruising on Loch Long. She was built by D. & W. Henderson in 1880 and for some of her career had a reputation as a teetotal steamer on which liquor was not sold. Problems with alcohol could sometime be an issue on paddle steamers, especially when a trip on a steamer was an annual treat. *Andrew Gladwell Collection*

instantly, did help to start the transport revolution for many. Any initial hesitation was short lived as the benefits became apparent. Soon, the growing prosperity created by the Industrial Revolution created a need for this money to be spent. A consumer society had been born. Leisure and pleasure now became a feature of life for some for the first time. People were now losing their reliance and somewhat limited focus on their own town. Travel was to become a core feature of the industrial age. The paddle steamer was part of that revolution that changed lives.

The early- to mid-nineteenth century was also a time when many of our largest seaside resorts grew from small villages by the sea to become large towns centred upon the hospitality and entertainment needs of their visitors. Seaside resorts were normally located close to one or more large concentrations of population. In most cases, these resorts would be easily accessible by paddle steamer, allowing passage to and from the resort in a day. Each major city of the industrial age had its own resort: London had Southend and Margate, Liverpool had Llandudno, Southampton had the Isle of Wight and Bournemouth whilst Glasgow had Dunoon and Rothesay. A fast and efficient means of reaching coastal towns was the prime requisite to prosperity. Coach travel of the past had done little to allow these towns to flourish. The paddle steamer became a catalyst for that change.

Paddle steamers started to develop routes very quickly. The largest and most developed resorts, although in their infancy, were obviously the most lucrative for operators but calls were also made at smaller places on the way to pick up more passengers to maximise revenue. Resorts quickly grew

**ABOVE** *Koh-i-Noor* at Clacton Pier. When paddle steamers got busier and resorts got bigger it was necessary for piers to be rebuilt to accommodate the steamer. This steamer was built by Fairfield in 1892 at a cost of £50,000. She was around 300ft in length and could accommodate 200 diners at a time. *Andrew Gladwell Collection*

up around paddle steamers and piers. It was natural for hotels, shops, and theatres to develop in the vicinity of each pier to maximise profit and to satisfy the needs of passengers. Paddle steamers significantly fuelled the seaside revolution. During the early period of paddle steamer operation in the UK, there was significant competition as rival local operators vied to become the most powerful. This often resulted in fierce demonstrations of aggressive behaviour that more often than not resulted in fights, tearing down of posters and considerable shouting to gather trade. This period of competition lasted until the 1880s when the key players had emerged and competition was more confined to developing steamers and routes.

The rise of the paddle steamer was dependent on the Industrial Revolution. New manufacturing processes combined with cheap, plentiful, skilled labour to make the production of

**ABOVE** London soon developed as a major centre for paddle steamers. The busy port with its close proximity to a vastly growing population enabled services to flourish. By the end of the century services had developed to include steamers such as this. The development of larger steamers meant that the Pool of London was often a navigational nightmare. *Ron Jones Collection*

FACING PAGE TOP *Princess of Wales* entered River Medway service in 1896. River Medway paddle steamers usually operated between the Medway Towns, Sheerness and Southend during Victorian times. *Princess of Wales* is shown here with Frindsbury in the distance. The Victorian era saw limited growth of Medway services, as steamers were small and suited to local services. *Andrew Gladwell Collection*

FACING PAGE BOTTOM *Lady of Lorne* was one of the early paddle steamers that plied the River Medway in Kent. Services principally operated between Chatham and Sheerness at the mouth of the river but developed later to the large seaside resort of Southend opposite Sheerness. *Andrew Gladwell Collection*

high-quality iron and steel achievable and affordable. Likewise, the design and manufacture of steam engines and advances in shipbuilding made the paddle steamer both economical and reliable. Raw materials such as coal could also be cheaply carried from the mines to the places where paddle steamers were located, to fuel the ever-hungry furnaces of the steamers. Everything came together during the nineteenth century and the paddle steamer gained a reputation for reliability, economy and performance that was hard to improve upon. It was a fusion that occurred almost simultaneously.

Paddle steamers during the mid and late Victorian period had strict rules on class segregation. In common with just about every other aspect of life at the time, passengers of different classes were kept apart from each other as far as was possible.

*'The steamers were very class conscious and passengers often grumbled at the number of ticket checks to ensure that passengers were separated by class. Often a man was placed at the dividing barrier rail to stop or surcharge any second class passenger proceeding aft.'* Edward Jones, 1898 (PSPS Collection)

Victorian paddle steamers differed significantly from what we would expect today, as facilities matched one's place in life. The rich middle classes were able to afford lavish saloons positioned in the best and roomiest areas of the paddle steamer. Their décor reflected the style of Victorian drawing rooms. The lower classes were provided with more basic wooden seating in the less pleasant areas of the steamer, usually below the waterline or having the poorest views of the scenery that they passed.

The widespread growth of railways in the UK during the 1830s and 1840s meant that paddle steamers quickly expanded their services to rival the trains. Railways provided opposition to the paddle steamer and themselves developed new resorts. They provided competition which in turn made each mode of transport improve its services. Despite railways being able to provide a fast and often

direct service, paddle steamers offered the advantage of providing quick links between resorts and towns either side of estuaries or between islands and the mainland. It was a distinct advantage of the paddle steamer that these links could be provided without the major building costs of bridges and tunnels. The paddle steamer just required a suitable landing place at each destination. The competition between railways and paddle steamers meant that resorts developed quickly and in most cases steamer and locomotive existed together. Inevitably, as services developed and technology and facilities advanced, passengers were conveyed greater distances. Advances in seaside pier design and construction ensured that piers could be built further out to sea to enable the new paddle steamers to land at all states of the tide.

As services developed and competition increased, steamers became larger and passenger accommodation became more comfortable. Most early paddle steamers were normally quite sparse with limited passenger facilities. Bars and refreshment facilities were often created with makeshift tables and saloons were limited by the size of the steamer. Profits from liquor made the steamer owners aware that handsome profits could be made from beer and refreshments as well as from tickets. Dining and bar facilities developed in this period and the potential for making money out of captive passengers whilst on a cruise was exploited with typical Victorian flair.

By the 1870s, the paddle steamer had developed to the point where the facilities, atmosphere, layout and size were more or less set for the decades that would follow.

## River Thames

London expanded dramatically during the early part of Victoria's reign. In 1820 the population of the city was one and a quarter million but by the end of the century, it had expanded to almost seven million. January 1815 saw the face of steam navigation on the river in London change when the paddle steamer *Marjory* arrived and she was soon joined by four new Thames paddle steamers. They opened up routes from London to Gravesend as well as to the more distant Margate. These early paddle steamers were called 'packets' and their primary role was to link places.

The pleasure gardens at Rosherville close to Gravesend became an early and popular leisure attraction. The more distant resorts of Southend and Margate were also early calling points and gained popularity, albeit slowly. Paddle steamer visits to Margate were frequently featured in the stirring paintings and sketches of J. M. W. Turner, who became a frequent visitor to the Kent resort. Places such as Southend, Herne Bay and Margate represented significant journeys if travelling by horse-drawn coach and sail vessels

ABOVE Wreckage of the *Princess Alice* was collected from the river banks after the steamer sunk. Souvenirs of the sinking were made from the debris such as this small trinket box with its handwritten inscription. Many of the passengers died from being poisoned by the raw sewage in the River Thames. *Andrew Gladwell*

LEFT The tragic sinking of the *Princess Alice* on the River Thames in 1878 caused widespread mourning at the hundreds of lives lost. Memorial cards were produced to commemorate the tragedy. It was noted that piles of bodies surrounded the exits from saloons on the vessel. This demonstrated that the steamer was heavily packed with passengers. *Andrew Gladwell Collection*

were dependent on tide and wind. The paddle steamer was revolutionary in that it offered the first opportunity to have a fast, cheap and reliable means of completing a journey quickly. By 1830s, it was said that 17 steamers were plying between London, Gravesend, Sheerness and Margate.

The most notable event during the period was the formation of the General Steam Navigation Company (GSNC) in 1824. By 1830, its importance was illustrated by the fact that it was operating five of the seventeen paddle steamers plying on the Thames. The names of two of these, *Royal Sovereign* and *Eagle*, would have a long history with the company.

Railways were part of the same transport revolution as the paddle steamers but developed a little later than the coastal steamers. With the opening of the South Eastern Railway's line to Margate from London Bridge and the London Bridge to Gravesend line in 1846, competition with the paddle steamers increased. In 1863 the Gravesend line

was extended to Chatham and Margate, thereby intensifying the rivalry. The construction of these railway lines proved a serious threat to the coastal steamers. The railways provided a wider number of stops along the route and were not dependant on the weather. Paddle steamers reacted by extending their services and facilities vigorously to provide competing services to the steam trains.

Paddle steamer services on the adjacent River Medway had a somewhat uneventful life during the Victorian era. The Medway Steam Packet Company, dating from 1837, primarily operated paddle steamers between Chatham and Sheerness. It later extended this service to the growing Essex resort of Southend on the other side of the Thames Estuary. By the 1870s, the company operated the *City of Rochester*, *Lady of Lorne* and *Alma* on Medway services.

The London Steamboat Company was formed in 1876 to provide amalgamated opposition to the GSNC. Prior to this, smaller operators competed with each other. The formation of the new company provided a formidable fleet of around 70 paddle steamers of all shapes and sizes. Some of its most notable steamers were *Alexandra*, *Albert Edward* and *Princess Alice*.

Just two years later, the *Princess Alice* gained widespread publicity for all of the wrong reasons. After several changes in ownership, she became part of the London Steamboat Company fleet. She was a large steamer and could carry up to 936 passengers between London and Gravesend. On 3 September 1878 she was returning from Gravesend with over 900 passengers onboard when the cargo steamer *Bywell Castle* struck the *Princess Alice* and sliced her in half, resulting in the steamer quickly sinking. There were no passenger records but it is thought that over 700 lives were lost. With typical Victorian emotion, parts of wreckage were fashioned into souvenirs and sold to remember those that had perished.

Despite the *Princess Alice* disaster, Thames paddle steamers continued to successfully ply the river and further paddle steamers were acquired from elsewhere. In 1885, the London Steamboat Company became part of the River Thames Steamboat Company. This resulted in several of the paddle steamers being disposed of, including the *Princess of Wales*, *Albert Edward* and *Alexandra*. This new company lasted only a few years until 1890 when it became part of the new Victoria Steamboat Association. By that time, a new era of intensified rivalry was about to erupt.

At Lulworth Cove.

## South Coast

South Coast services were dominated by Cosens and Red Funnel. Both companies were formed in the mid-Victorian era and continued to lead paddle steamer services for a century. Cosens was founded in 1852 by Captain James Cosens and J. Drew and was based at Weymouth, initially to operate services between Weymouth and neighbouring Portland. Cosens' early steamers included *Princess*, *Highland Maid* and *Wave Queen*. Cosens encountered competition from John Tizard who operted *Premier* and *Bannockburn* at Weymouth before amalgamating with Cosens in 1876. *Premier* became part of the Cosens fleet and had a long and distinguished career with them. Such frenzies of competition benefited the expansion and enrichment of services as they ensured that competitors engaged new tonnage, increased passenger comfort and initiated new routes. In 1879, Cosens took delivery of the *Empress*. This was a time of great growth for Weymouth as the paddle steamers enabled more and more services to link with destinations such as Bournemouth and Swanage and both resorts also expanded as a result.

A natural centre for paddle steamer services was the Isle of Wight, due to its geographical location and much-needed ferry links to the mainland. In 1861, the longest-named and longest-surviving steamer operator commenced

**ABOVE** *Empress* was an early member of the Cosens fleet and plied the Dorset Coast until the mid-1950s. *Empress* was built by Samuda Brothers of Poplar in 1879. Cosens steamers were well-known for their local trips to places such as Lulworth Cove, as here. *Andrew Gladwell Collection*

services when the Isle of Wight & South of England Royal Mail Steam Packet Company (commonly known as Red Funnel) placed its first paddle steamers in service. The fleet soon grew with the introduction of the *Southampton*, *Prince Leopold* and *Carisbrooke*. The company's principal route was between Southampton and Isle of Wight piers such as those at Cowes, Ryde and Yarmouth. The period of expansion coincided with the heyday of the Isle of Wight as the holiday and weekend home of Queen Victoria. The resorts and steamer services quickly grew to cope with the Victorian exploitation of the island. The company had two roles. The first was to maintain the ferry link with the mainland and the second was to provide a number of attractive excursions round the island and to the mainland during the busy summer months. Most of the steamers were dual purpose and could act as ferry and excursion vessels. A number of smaller paddle steamers supplemented excursion services during the summer.

ABOVE *Comet* at Weymouth. She was a wooden paddle tug and
operated on the Swanage and Poole service. She was typical of
the early paddle tugs in her small size and lack of facilities.
Paddle tugs often combined towage work with excursion sailings.
*PSPS Collection*

BELOW *Telegraph* was a Poole paddle tug that operated to Weymouth
during the early 1880s. She undertook towage tasks as well as
offering excursion work and services between Poole and Swanage
for a time. Cosens provided a vital ferry service between Weymouth
and nearby Portland. *PSPS Collection*

**ABOVE** Paddle steamers of the Cosens fleet plied for trade along the Dorset coast as well as to and from the Isle of Wight. The company never invested in revolutionary new steamers and made do with many old and small vessels. *PSPS Collection*

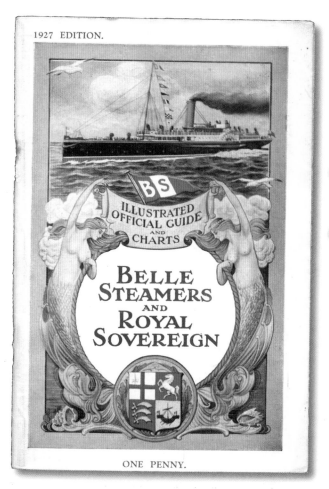

**ABOVE** The Cosens fleet was based at Weymouth and provided paddle steamer services along the Dorset Coast and further afield for over a century. Its distinctive house flag was shown on crockery, uniforms, handbills and other publicity material. *PSPS Collection*

**LEFT** Steamer companies soon became aware of the value of attractive publicity material. Cheap printing ensured that posters, handbills and brochures could be easily produced to advertise services. *John Gilmore*

**ABOVE** The Firth of Clyde was unique in the UK as it had many remote islands and calling points. Garelochhead was an example of one of the great number of small piers that were built to connect these places to the larger piers and towns. Piers such as those at Rothesay and Dunoon were particularly large and busy and many incorporated signalling equipment to tell steamers when to berth. *John Gilmore Collection*

**ABOVE** *Grenadier* was built for the David MacBrayne fleet in 1885. During the summer months she undertook the famous Oban to Staffa and Iona service. Passengers are shown here landing from her by boat at Fingal's Cave, Staffa. *Ron Jones Collection*

## Firth of Clyde

Paddle steamers were able to reach the centre of Glasgow, and therefore they were the best and easiest way to reach towns on the Firth of Clyde and along the Ayrshire coast in the days before the railways were built. Railway services were developed on the Firth of Clyde during the 1830s and 1840s, but paddle steamers quickly enhanced the services provided by the railways to give fast crossings across the Firth of Clyde to link the many islands and harbours that were impossible to reach by the railway alone. Paddle steamers and their excellent links with the railways ensured success and timetables were produced to reflect these links. Glasgow folk quickly developed a deep love and appreciation of the beauties of the nearby Firth of Clyde viewed from a paddle steamer.

Although it was sensible for Firth of Clyde operators to link steamer and railway services, as these would mutually benefit each other, the Government was not so keen on this. It attempted to stop railway companies operating paddle steamers and early attempts met with failure. In 1866, the North British Railway company started a steamer service from Helensburgh to Ardrishaig with the paddle steamers *Meg Merrilies* and *Dandie Dinmont* but the service soon failed.

The origins of David MacBrayne stretch back to 1851 when it was formed to operate steamer services to the West Highlands. Its paddle steamer named *Columba* was one of the finest ever built. At over 300 feet in length, she catered for the most affluent of passengers during the summer months, with another paddle steamer, the *Grenadier*, providing the important mail service during the winter months.

This period witnessed the entry into service of some of the most famous and well-loved Clyde steamers. One of these was the *Ivanhoe*. Built as a teetotal steamer, she operated to Arran via Bute and was particularly favoured by families who could be guaranteed a cruise without the more lively behaviour of male passengers brought on by the consumption of vast amounts of liquor.

The Campbell family was a popular operator of paddle steamers on the Clyde, with a service between the Broomielaw at Glasgow and the Holy Loch. Despite financial problems, Captain Campbell was able to purchase the *Meg Merrilies*. Together with his sons Peter and Alec, the family was able to build a fine and profitable fleet with *Waverley* and later the *Madge Wildfire*. By the late 1880s, after Captain Campbell died, the rising threat of the railway

**ABOVE** Thomas Telford designed the vast steamer quays at the Broomielaw at Glasgow, which were always a lively place for pleasure steamers arriving and departing as folk were taken 'Doon the Watter', particularly during 'Glasgow Fair'. In this view *Iona* is canting and *Benmore* is alongside the quay. *John Gilmore Collection*

companies became a massive problem, Peter and Alec realised what would happen and in 1888 relocated their business from the Firth of Clyde to the Bristol Channel, taking the *Waverley* with them.

The Caledonian Railway Company then inaugurated its Clyde service. It had purchased the *Madge Wildfire* and *Meg Merrilies* from the Campbell family when it moved south. Both of these successful steamers provided the foundation of a good fleet. There was strong opposition from many quarters, however, and the company was forced to form an associate company to operate the paddle steamer fleet. This resulted in the Caledonian Steam Packet Company being formed in 1889.

Paddle steamers were able to quickly link Glasgow and other large towns and ports with the growing seaside resorts required by the Victorian masses, such as Rothesay. Merchants and businessmen were also able to commute quickly between their work and their pleasant newly-built homes on picturesque loch-side shores distant from the boisterous city. Mail and goods could now also be carried quickly and efficiently to many of these destinations for the first time by paddle steamer.

Quite soon, the tradition of going 'Doon the Watter' was started. Glasgow had a long history of celebrating annual fairs and 'Glasgow Fair' soon became synonymous with paddle steamers. Vast numbers of Glaswegians would board the paddle steamers at the Broomielaw or would catch a steam train to the coast to connect with a steamer. With an abundance of attractive harbours and bays, the Firth of Clyde provided a plethora of seaside resorts for the visitor. Places such as Rothesay, Largs, Dunoon and Ayr saw a great boom in popularity. Rothesay grew to be the most popular destination as it was relatively close to Glasgow and therefore offered a quick destination at an affordable price.

As well as the major tourist destinations, the Firth of Clyde also offered a number of smaller calling points. At these, a small pier would provide access with a small village. A limited amount of holiday accommodation was available but in the main, these locations were mainly for wealthy businessmen who built impressive villas along the shore.

## Lancashire Coast

Fleetwood offered pleasure cruises as early as 1840. Originally planned as a grand seaside resort, Sir Peter Hesketh-Fleetwood saw paddle steamers as an important aspect of his town's growth. Trips were offered by such vessels as *Cupid* and *Express* which had arrived at Fleetwood in 1840. From 1843, *Nile* offered cruises to Glasson Dock, Piel Island and Bardsea and by 1846, *Ayrshire Lassie* had also entered service.

The Victorian boom in pier building was the catalyst that promoted an explosion of steamer services along the Lancashire coast. Growth in the recreational opportunities offered by the developing resorts, fuelled by expanding

**FACING PAGE TOP** *Clifton* at Blackpool North Pier. The pier was designed by the famous Victorian pier builder – Engenius Birch. This early view shows the steamer alongside the original pier head. This was later significantly enlarged to house a theatre and concert room as well as a vast landing jetty required by larger steamers after significant silting. *Andrew Gladwell Collection*

**FACING PAGE BELOW** Paddle steamer services exploded on the Lancashire coast when large piers started to be built in the mid-1860s. This coincided with the widespread development of the railway system and the growth of resorts such as Blackpool and Southport. *Andrew Gladwell Collection*

**ABOVE** Southport Pier is not remembered as a destination for paddle steamers these days. Southport, along with close-by resorts such as Lytham and St Annes, experienced a very short life as calling points as sands caused significant problems. Several small Morecambe Bay piers also suffered the same fate. *Andrew Gladwell Collection*

**LEFT** Wine and spirit list for the North Pier Steamship Company of Blackpool. The sale of liquor was always lucrative for paddle steamer operators. North Pier steamers tended to attract more refined passengers whilst the Central Pier attracted a more boisterous working class clientele. *Andrew Gladwell Collection*

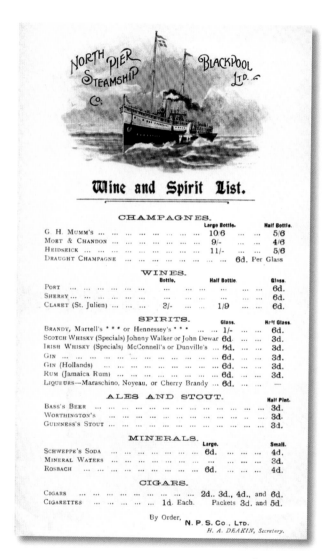

train services and the Bank Holidays Act of 1871, gave many of the working classes of the Lancashire mill towns the opportunity to take a day trip to the seaside for the first time. The 'Wakes Week' soon became part of the life of each seaside town. Ship owners and other entrepreneurs were quick to react to the potential of this market. Soon, converted tugs and other temporary vessels took up the role of pleasure steamers out of Blackpool, Morecambe, Southport, St Annes and Barrow but it was not until the opening of Blackpool North Pier in 1863 that services really started to flourish.

*Wellington* entered service at Blackpool in 1871 and had a passenger certificate for 350 and a rather limiting speed of just 10 knots. She usually sailed to Morecambe and Southport, but would occasionally venture as far as Llandudno. She had as a contemporary, the *Clifton*, owned by the North Pier Company. A little later, the North Pier Company acquired the *Queen of the Bay*. The first known steamers to operate services from the Central Pier were the *Minnow*, *Lion* and *Dandy*. They were Liverpool-owned boats that made their way to Blackpool during the months of July, August and September during the late 1860s and early 1870s. Although not fitted out to the later luxurious standards of Blackpool pleasure steamers, they provided the much-needed trips to Southport and Morecambe as well as short cruises for those that did not relish the more lively sailings. The first real pleasure steamer built for the Central Pier was the *Bickerstaffe* of 1879.

By the end of the 1870s, the shifting sands off of the piers necessitated the construction of expensive and huge jetties several hundred of feet in length so that paddle steamers could gain access at all stages of the tide. Such work was a heavy burden for the Lancashire Coast steamers and this, combined with exposure to the often harsh weather conditions of the Irish Sea, meant that pleasure steamer services in the region would never develop to their full potential.

# 2

# The Heyday of the Paddle Steamer

**ABOVE** *Jeanie Deans* at Rothesay early in her career. *Jeanie Deans* was built for the
London and North Eastern Railway by Fairfield of Govan in 1931 to provide competition
to the *Duchess of Montrose*. Her shallow draft enabled her to visit Craigendoran and
Helensburgh. Her name recalled that of an earlier steamer and carried on the tradition
of the North British Railway of naming its steamers after characters from
Sir Walter Scott's novels. *PSPS Collection*

The celebrations for Queen Victoria's Diamond Jubilee in 1897 were the high point of the heyday of the paddle steamer. By then, the key operators had evolved around our coastline and the most popular cruising routes were established. In fact, the paddle steamer would never see such an extensive area of cruising again. The design of the classic British paddle steamer was also more or less confirmed and operators felt supremely confident in their fleets and their future. The market for the cruises provided by these steamers was also well established and appeared to be ever-increasing.

P. & A. CAMPBELL, Ltd.

Royal Naval Review, Spithead.

Her Majesty's Diamond Jubilee.

⊹ 1897. ⊹

LEFT Ticket for Queen Victoria's Royal Naval Review at Spithead to mark her Diamond Jubilee in 1897. The event saw the greatest ever assembly of ships and countless paddle steamers from all over the UK attended. Twenty-one battleships and 53 cruisers as well as numerous pleasure steamers and small vessels were present. *PSPS Collection*

By the 1890s, the paddle steamer had evolved to the point that would make it familiar to passengers several generations later and, indeed, many of the steamers that entered service in the 1890s were to last until services sharply declined in the middle of the 20th century. Advances in engineering design and production had led to the development of steam engines that were reliable and perfectly suited to their role. Steel manufacture and shipbuilding had also reached their peak at shipyards located at places such as the Clyde, Tyne and Thames. Many famous yards such as Denny Brothers, Fairfield and John Thornycroft became well-established specialist builders of paddle steamers. They created large and impressive vessels that were built specifically for the areas that they were to serve.

The typical design of a paddle steamer had also evolved. By this time, operators had seen that passengers required ample, well-appointed facilities far superior to the sparse conditions of the early years. Operators also became aware that their prestige could be reflected in the quality of décor aboard the steamers. As the number of steamers and competition increased, the frenzy of change was reflected in the size and luxury of the paddle steamers being built, epitomising the transport revolution that occurred during the Victorian Age.

BELOW Navigation was somewhat difficult in the days before radar. Here the *Cambria* lies aground on rocks just outside Ilfracombe harbour in July 1926. Such incidents seemed to be quite profitable for local boatmen as well as photographers who published postcards of such mishaps. *Ron Jones Collection*

P.S. "CAMBRIA"
ASHORE NR ILFRACOMBE.
JULY 12TH 1926. No 105.

Landing Passengers, Clovelly

**ABOVE** Passengers were usually able to land on a pier from a paddle steamer. At more remote locations, a small boat was used to ferry people ashore and a precarious plank was often used to make the final few steps to the beach. *Ron Jones Collection*

**LEFT** *Royal Sovereign* was part of the New Palace Steamer fleet. She was built by the famous Fairfield yard in 1893 and was over 300ft in length, with telescopic funnels to enable her to manoeuvre under London Bridge in the days before Tower Pier was built. She had several owners at a time where there was a great deal of competition and was finally sold to the GSNC for £5,540 and operated by them in 1929. *Andrew Gladwell Collection*

The paddle steamers reached something of a 'Golden Age' during the Edwardian era. It was a time when it looked as if nothing could ever change. The confidence of the time was matched by an ever-increasing number of passengers that flocked aboard paddle steamers at each pier with a landing arm. Inevitably, times of prosperity are always matched by periods of change and challenge. After the outbreak of World War 1 many of the young men seen posing in evocative on-deck photographs a few years previously would be slaughtered in the wartime trenches. The world would never be quite the same again.

*'Following the Titanic disaster of 1912, 1913 saw the introduction of additional lifesaving apparatus which included extra boats and some form of appliance for everyone on board. I remember making the* Yarmouth Belle's *first trip in early May to Margate with work in progress. Stanchions were fitted for the extra boats and there was a large stack of life-belts on the bridge behind the wheel.'* (Edward Smith, PSPS Collection)

*'1914 was the last season of the "Paddlers' Heyday". Sailings proceeded normally until the outbreak of hostilities. They were then somewhat confused and gradually dropped off.*

*There were press adverts stating "We are still running" for a time as would be passengers didn't know whether to turn up or not.'* (Edward Smith, PSPS Collection)

The years immediately before the outbreak of World War 1 saw a number of withdrawals and changes in the fleets. It was a period of change due to considerable competition.

*'Motor cars, bikes and charabancs began to appear and were a menace to the steamers. Rail services were also improving and taking an increasing share of the trade.'* (c1912 Thames, PSPS Collection)

The introduction of a new steamer normally meant that one would be withdrawn elsewhere. It was a simple economic fact that, although buoyant, trade could only support a certain amount of passengers. At this time, fleets in some areas were up to strength, especially on the Firth of Clyde and South Coast. Despite there being a glut of serviceable but unwanted paddle steamers for sale, the places where they could be transferred and operated was contracting especially as other operators often preferred to build new steamers to their own specification to demonstrate their dominance in an area.

ABOVE The end of the Edwardian period saw many changes in the paddle steamer fleets around the UK. Many large steamers such as *La Marguerite* were moved to new areas. She was never a profitable steamer for her original owners on the Thames due to her size and hunger for coal but her sale to the Liverpool & North Wales Steamship Company enabled her to be operated more profitably as coal and labour were cheaper there. *Andrew Gladwell Collection*

RIGHT Brochures often projected a glamorous and stylish image of their steamers. The 1930s Art Deco style allowed P. & A. Campbell to show its luxurious steamers to best effect in this brochure for the Sussex Coast. It advertised day trips to France where passengers had four hours ashore. *Ron Jones*

The years following the end of World War 1 saw many old steamers refitted, emerging to take up the reins of summer operation once again.

*'There was a revival of paddler sailings after the First World War ended, but those great days and pleasures of the pre-war decade never returned in anything like the same measure.'* (c1920 South Coast, PSPS Collection)

By the 1920s the effects of competition and changes in technology and in people's lives in general began to affect the world of the paddle steamer. Competition was now resulting in an increasing number of the larger steamers being placed in service in new operating areas. Many others were simply withdrawn and scrapped. Some were also beginning to be replaced by more modern propeller-driven steamers which, in the inevitable march of progress, would one day replace the traditional paddle steamer. It was clear that the heyday of the paddle steamer had passed its peak.

The 1930s would see those trends develop further. The decade would also see a fundamental shift in the lives of people in the UK as changes such as the Holidays with Pay Act of 1938 came into force. The increase in leisure time in the decade led to a wider range of leisure activities becoming available to the public. For the first time, a day at the seaside by paddle steamer was not the only option.

## London and the River Thames

By the late 1880s, the Thames-based General Steam Navigation Company was facing increased competition and its fleet needed updating. The effect of competition was often beneficial to services and this certainly was the case on the Thames. GSNC reacted to opposition from the River Thames Steamboat Company by building five large 'Bird' class' steamers in the 1880s. These were modern steamers, each with impressive saloons that reached the full width of the steamer. They looked magnificent, with *Philomel* being the largest.

At the same time, the resorts of the East Coast such as Clacton, Walton and Felixstowe were gaining an appetite to obtain some of the lucrative market offered by London. Paddle steamer services were developed in these resorts and, coinciding with the massive expansion of the GSNC fleet, investors on the East Coast built their own impressive fleet of 'Belle' steamers. Between 1890 and 1896, four new steamers were built for the Thames and East Coast excursion trade: *Clacton Belle*, *Woolwich Belle*, *London Belle* and *Southend Belle*. Each steamer was resplendent, with the

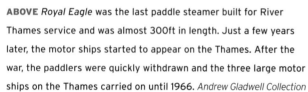

ABOVE *Royal Eagle* was the last paddle steamer built for River Thames service and was almost 300ft in length. Just a few years later, the motor ships started to appear on the Thames. After the war, the paddlers were quickly withdrawn and the three large motor ships on the Thames carried on until 1966. *Andrew Gladwell Collection*

ABOVE Great Yarmouth was the most northerly point for steamers of the GSNC and Belle Steamer fleets. A custom in pre-World War 1 days was the 'husband's boat'. This was a time when the working week ended at lunchtime on Saturday rather than on Friday evening. Special services were laid on which sailed on the Saturday afternoon and returned on the Sunday afternoon, enabling husbands to join their wives and children at the coast. *Andrew Gladwell Collection*

name of one of the fleet's calling points to create a recognisable brand. Such a venture had to meet with some success and in 1897 the well-loved company Belle Steamers was formed. The fleet was a notable but short-lived success story on the River Thames. The owning company was canny in that it owned the piers as well as a grand hotel, making it to a great extent self-sufficient.

The venerable General Steam Navigation Company also faced competition from another company on the Thames, the New Palace Steamers. The 1890s was not a calm decade for paddle steamers on the Thames!

*'I remember the excitement at London Bridge in the mornings with touting. The GSNC and New Palace companies each set up pitches with tents to vie with each other to capture the trade of intending passengers. Prospective passengers were pestered by the touts to book for "their" steamer – "The First to get to Margate", "Fastest and Best boat in the River". On a busy Saturday or Sunday morning there was real fun in*

**LEFT** *Crested Eagle* approaching Clacton Pier on the first day of the 1939 season. For that year only, she had been given a large and bold observation saloon in front of the funnel. This replaced an earlier wooden one that was much more in keeping with the look of the steamer. *Andrew Gladwell*

**ABOVE** *Walton Belle* was part of the famed Belle Steamer fleet. This view shows a typical arrival of a paddle steamer at a pier. Deck crew can be seen ready with ropes to secure the bow whilst other crew are standing on the sponson with mooring ropes. Finally, the helmsman is positioning the steamer. *PSPS Collection*

**BELOW** *London Belle* at Clacton Pier. The famed Denny of Dumbarton yard built the Belle fleet. The *London Belle*, with her large fixed funnel, was the largest of the fleet and became serious competition to the *Koh-I-Noor*. She was a fast steamer and had ample luxurious saloons with electric light. *Andrew Gladwell Collection*

LEFT A short-lived enterprise on the Thames was that of the London County Council paddle steamers. This huge fleet of 30 paddle steamers was built to provide a service linking a large number of piers in the centre of London. Within three years, the service had ceased. This admirable venture had been undermined by the expansion of the electric tramway system in London – a system that was promoted by the London County Council! *Andrew Gladwell Collection*

ABOVE Tower Bridge has been a central point for pleasure steamer cruises to and from London since it opened in 1894. Most of the GSNC paddle steamers would turn before they reached the bridge and would then operate stern-first to Tower Pier. This enabled them to be ready for service the next day. Up to eight tons of stores were needed each day so time was always at a premium. *Andrew Gladwell Collection*

ABOVE When *Kingfisher* was introduced on Thames services in 1906 she was a new departure for the General Steam Navigation Company, being a turbine steamer. Her career on the Thames was short-lived and just a few years after she was introduced the company brought back paddle steamers. *Andrew Gladwell Collection*

*watching the various antics . . . "Pay here for the* Eagle *– fastest and cheapest" or "Travel by* Royal Sovereign *– book with us and enjoy the comfort of a really luxurious and first class ship".* (Edward Smith, PSPS Collection)

The first decade of the 20th century was an era when confidence in the industry was at an all time high and the Thames fleet was perhaps at its most magnificent. When Edward VII ascended the throne in 1901, there were 20 pleasure steamers operating on the river. This was, of course far too many for the trade that existed. Before the onset of World War 1, several of these steamers were withdrawn.

One of the first large steamers to go was the majestic *La Marguerite* in 1903. The Fairfield company, as well as having involvement on the Thames, had interests in the growing North Wales trade from Liverpool and it was inevitable that it would transfer this coal-hungry steamer to an area where there was less competition. This resulted in a far leaner fleet with which to battle against the mighty GSNC and Belle Steamer fleets.

GSNC reacted to the competition by getting rid of the older, less economic steamers and replacing them as much as possible with new tonnage. Unexpectedly, in 1906 it introduced a turbine steamer named *Kingfisher*. It also replaced two of its 'Bird' class' steamers. By this time, these steamers had become dated and had limited modern passenger requisites such as electric light. The disposal of these older steamers on the Thames greatly refreshed the steamer fleets of other cruising areas around the UK where they were redeployed. Companies in these areas could choose from a great number of attractive second-hand paddle steamers that could be easily purchased. The variety and charm of these vessels made them ideal for shorter scenic voyages as well as for less important and therefore more economic routes.

*'I was determined to reach Boulogne before the end of 1911. Quite alone, I made a long day trip and spent under £1. I took the 7.15am from Croydon to Hastings and picked up the* Brighton Queen *for Boulogne. After three hours in France I returned to*

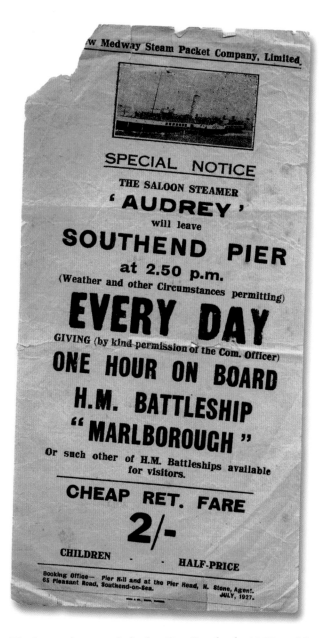

*Hastings and got a train back to East Croydon by 11.15pm. My mother, bless her, thought I had done something wonderful and told the neighbours that her son had been abroad, to France, and back all in a day!'* (T. More, PSPS Collection)

1909 was a momentous year for Thames steamers when the *Golden Eagle* entered service. Built by the famous John Brown yard on the Clyde, she became known as the most elegant and good looking of all of the Thames steamers.

*'Racing on the Thames was taboo but in 1909* Golden Eagle *arrived and sometimes we got a run for Margate. Four vessels would converge near the Nore and each hoped to get to Margate first for "first in" was ahead for the rest of the day. I have known occasions when the chief engineer would look down into the stoke-hold of "Kohy" and tell the boys to give him more steam. If there was a beer in it, did they shovel!'* (T. More, PSPS Collection)

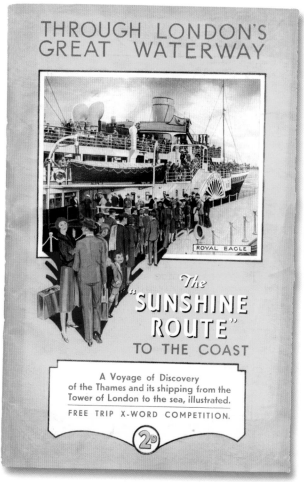

**ABOVE** *Crested Eagle* was part of the GSNC fleet and was known as 'The Greyhound of the River'. She was built with a collapsible funnel and mast to allow her to pass under London Bridge (a few years after she entered service Tower Pier was built to stop paddlers having to pass under the bridge). Her master Captain Cole always wore white kid gloves and was known for his very high standards. *Andrew Gladwell Collection*

**LEFT** Paddle steamers were often described as 'butterfly boats'. This may be due to the fact that they flitted between seaside piers or because they looked like butterflies from above. The *Crested Eagle* shows her wide sponson area in this view taken from the *Royal Eagle* whilst alongside Southend Pier. *Andrew Gladwell Collection*

**ABOVE** *Royal Eagle* was known as 'London's Luxury Liner' when she was introduced in 1932. She had a target audience of the more affluent classes and her fares could be three times more than the older *Golden Eagle*. She had been built by Cammell Laird and provided significant comfort to her 1,987 passengers with her large crew of 70. Her massive undercover accommodation was the largest ever on a pleasure steamer. *PSPS Collection*

After the end of World War 1, it was the turn of the River Medway fleet of the New Medway Steam Packet Company to expand. The original prewar company had in its fleet several aged paddle steamers. With the formation of the 'New' company came an ambitious new director – Captain Sidney Shippick. From the modest beginnings of the Strood to Southend service, the company soon ventured further afield to places as far away as Great Yarmouth and to France. 1924 marked a defining year for the company when the *Medway Queen* entered service on the Medway and Thames.

The next year, 1925, saw the first appearance on the Thames of one of the most distinctive of all paddle steamers – the *Crested Eagle*. She was one of the last paddle steamers that had to contend with Old Swan Pier at London and therefore had to go under London Bridge. Just a few years later, Tower Pier was constructed and steamers such as *Crested Eagle* could then call there; the need for a collapsible funnel and mast disappeared. She had the nickname of 'Greyhound of the Thames' and could attain a speed of 20 knots.

Shippick continued his programme of introducing new steamers throughout the late 1920s and early 1930s. These included the acquisition of ex-Navy vessels as well as those from Thames competitors. Services were also expanded due

to improved landing facilities at piers. The most impressive of these was the construction of the Prince George Extension to Southend Pier in 1929.

In 1932 another distinctive paddle steamer was introduced to the Thames when the *Royal Eagle* entered service for GSNC, operating from London. She became the last large paddle steamer built for Thames service. *Royal Eagle* looked significantly different to earlier Thames paddle steamers as she had extensive sun lounges and saloons on top of her promenade deck, unlike earlier Thames steamers that had mainly open decks. GSNC was aware that her passengers required more luxurious undercover accommodation than their forefathers demanded and that they also wanted accommodation that gave them a good view as they travelled to the coast, and therefore the vast sun lounges were built to satisfy these needs. The future would, however, lie with a more sleek and revolutionary type of vessel.

**ABOVE** The Queen Line of pleasure steamers was the brainchild of Sidney Shippick who revolutionised the services of the New Medway Steam Packet Company from the 1920s onwards. The fleet grew massively during the interwar years with many new steamers being introduced. *Andrew Gladwell Collection*

Also in 1932 the New Medway Steam Packet Company started a direct run from London and in the following year competition with GSNC intensified when the Medway company introduced a day return trip from London to Felixstowe as well as one from London to the Thanet resorts. Along with services to the continent from Clacton and Gravesend, it was clear that the Medway company was increasingly becoming a real threat to the dominant GSNC.

The New Medway Company continued to acquire more vessels and to subtly introduce new services or to tweak old ones. The company purchased older paddle steamers and motor vessels from elsewhere but often they lasted only a

**RIGHT** The main dining saloon of the *Royal Eagle* in 1947. Huge numbers of diners could be served and meals were at timed sittings. The steamer was oil fired and oil was also used in the galley to cook the breakfast, luncheon and dinner which were served on the steamer – lobster was a favourite with diners! *Andrew Gladwell Collection*

short while before they disappeared again and moved on into service with other companies.

*'The purser was a big powerful ex-policeman who was most likeable and a gentle chap. If any of our beer drinkers got "out of hand", Bob was a very useful man to have around. Occasionally we had drunks who had to be carried ashore. One of Bob's favourites was to come round the ship shortly before reaching Southend chanting "Any more for Southend on mud…get ready for landing at Southend on Mud!"'* (Edward Smith, PSPS Collection)

The New Medway Steam Packet Company showed its confidence and power when it introduced a revolution on the Thames in 1935 with the construction of the motor vessel *Queen of the Channel*. The introduction of other steamers from elsewhere to build up a Medway and Thames service had given the company a very significant knowledge of operating steamers and a very clear indication of what the public wanted. The building of new cinemas, housing and modern seaside palaces of pleasure in Art Deco style showed that there was an appetite for a bold fresh style. There had also been a shift towards passengers requiring accommodation that was more comfortable and spacious than before. The grand and sometimes stuffy Victorian and Edwardian interiors that screamed about the statuses of the owners now needed to be more tailored to passenger comfort than prestige.

The famed Denny of Dumbarton yard built the revolutionary *Queen of the Channel*. Her propulsion was by diesel engine and she could attain 19 knots in service. In common with newly built steamers of the time, she had

extensive covered passenger accommodation on her promenade deck that gave passengers excellent facilities.

The introduction of the *Queen of the Channel* of course intensified the competition between the NMSPC and the GSNC. The New Medway Steam Packet Company dealt a significant second blow when it ordered a new diesel vessel in 1936. The GSNC reacted by quickly buying up shares of the Medway company, and the two companies merged. The new ship was named *Royal Sovereign* and was a larger version of the *Queen of the Channel*. A novel feature that was developed on this particular steamer was the building of side 'blisters' on her hull that flared the hull out in the midships section. Amusingly, this gave this revolutionary new diesel vessel the look and interior space of a paddle steamer. These 'blisters' allowed deck houses and saloons to be built wide across the decks to provide extensive passenger accommodation. An era of fast and comfortable travel on modern vessels had now arrived.

**ABOVE** *Queen of Kent* and *Queen of Thanet* were two former World War 1 minesweepers acquired by the New Medway Steam Packet Company. They had a distinctive look with their two thin funnels. *Andrew Gladwell Collection*

THE CRESTED EAGLE

**RIGHT** A 1930s souvenir from the *Crested Eagle*. River Thames services during that decade witnessed great changes. Paddle steamers like the *Crested Eagle* were still relatively new but were faced with the sleek modern motor ships that entered service during the middle of the decade. *PSPS Collection*

**BELOW** Thames services were invigorated with the arrival of the *Royal Sovereign* and *Queen of the Channel* during the mid-1930s. They typified the style and ambience of the age and offered splendid cruises for Londoners. They provided popular services to France and Belgium as well as to the coast. *Andrew Gladwell Collection*

**ABOVE** *Queen of the Channel* was built for Thames and Continental service during the mid-1930s and typified the confidence of the times in the future of Thames pleasure steamer cruising. She was originally going to be called *Continental Queen*. She bore some similarity to the *Queen Mary* of the Clyde. Her life was short as she was lost during World War 2. *Andrew Gladwell Collection*

The Thames motor ships of the 1930s and 1940s had revolutionary 'blisters' at their sides to increase the width of the ship and to give greater passenger accommodation. Many thought that these looked like a sponson on a paddle steamer. *Andrew Gladwell Collection*

**LEFT** The mid to late 1930s saw the introduction of sleek new motor ships to most areas. They reflected the style of the age as well as using new and more efficient methods of propulsion. Attractive and colourful publicity marketed these new steamers well. *Andrew Gladwell Collection*

**ABOVE** *Royal Daffodil* entered Thames service in May 1939. She was built by Denny of Dumbarton and provided a bold pre-war statement of the confidence of the Eagle & Queen Line. She could carry up to 2,063 passengers at 21 knots. *Andrew Gladwell Collection*

**ABOVE** The white-funnelled paddle steamers of the P. & A. Campbell fleet made it one of the most distinctive fleets in the UK for over seven decades. *Britannia* and *Cambria* are shown here departing from Ilfracombe. The resort was hugely popular with Campbell passengers and became the principal resort of the Bristol Channel. *PSPS Collection*

**ABOVE** Cover for 'Now and Then', the Eagle & Queen Line illustrated guide for 1939. Most operating companies published high quality guides to entice their passengers and to promote future business. This particular brochure contained artist-drawn images to show what travel was like in the early days compared to the luxury of the 1930s. *Andrew Gladwell Collection*

After the GSNC and NMSP merged, steamers and services were trimmed and altered to provide a more economic pattern of service on the Thames. Although World War 2 was imminent and would affect the Thames fleet forever, there was one final pleasure steamer to defiantly enter service on the London river. Perhaps one of the most fondly-remembered steamers of all entered service in 1939, just a few months before war was declared. *Royal Daffodil* was a magnificent pleasure steamer. She was much bigger than her two older sisters and offered the best passenger accommodation imaginable. She was the epitome of the modern age.

### Bristol Channel

Peter and Alec Campbell were well known for successfully operating steamers on the Clyde before they moved south to the Bristol Channel during the late 1880s. Their steamer *Waverley* departed from the Clyde in May 1887 and became an immediate success, showing the potential of operating a steamer on the Bristol Channel between Bristol and Ilfracombe and at places between the two ports.

The Campbell family relocated to the Bristol Channel completely at the end of 1888. Bristol at this time was a flourishing port and centre of commerce and the sleek white paddle steamers of the Campbell fleet were very popular with Bristolians. Others were of course recognising the potential for business in Bristol and competition from Cardiff-based operators soon became a problem. P. & A. Campbell always had magnificent local support and this

LEFT P. & A. Campbell's *Cambria* was built in 1896 and conformed to the Campbell style of having a wide uncluttered promenade deck from bow to stern. Her sisters *Britannia* and *Westward Ho* that were both built at the same time had a similar appearance. *PSPS Collection*

BELOW The Barry Railway's *Westonia* and *Gwalia* at Cardiff. *Westonia* had a long and complicated career including spells on the South Coast and in North Wales as well as in the Bristol Channel. *Gwalia* was later sold for service with the Furness Railway and renamed *Lady Moyra*. After the failure of that venture, she returned to Bristol Channel service for Tuckers. *Andrew Gladwell Collection*

ABOVE P. & A. Campbell's *Britannia* entered Bristol Channel service in 1896 and was a particularly good-looking paddle steamer. She became the flagship of the Campbell fleet from her introduction until the introduction of the *Bristol Queen* some 50 years later. *PSPS Collection*

BELOW The lounge aboard P. & A. Campbell's famous *Britannia*. Operating companies always ensured that the interior spaces of their steamers reflected their ambitions. Saloons and dining facilities were stylish and comfortable and equalled the facilities and ambience of good hotels. *Ron Jones Collection*

**ABOVE** *Westward Ho* at Ilfracombe in 1911. Paddle steamers were typically secured to a pier with ropes at each end and at small platforms either side of the paddle box. These ropes were used to 'cant' or position the steamer by putting power on the rope. *Westward Ho* was built by S. McKnight & Co of Ayr in 1894 and was the first Bristol Channel steamer to have a promenade deck reaching to the bow. *Ian Saunders Collection*

**BELOW** The crew of P. & A. Campbell's *Glen Usk*. Crew were normally seasonal and many in the catering department found employment in the off-season winter months in hotels and restaurants in the big cities. Over one hundred people could be employed on some paddle steamers. *Ian Saunders Collection*

encouraged the company to build a new steamer for Bristol Channel services. The first P. & A. Campbell Bristol Channel paddle steamer was the *Ravenswood* of 1891. This was met by the introduction of *Lorna Doone* by competitors. Campbell's popularity and confidence grew even more and soon introduced excursions run in conjunction with the Midland Railway which greatly increased the number of passengers using its services.

P. & A. Campbell introduced three superb new steamers between 1894 and 1896 when *Westward Ho*, *Cambria* and *Britannia* entered service. The most distinctive feature of these was a long and impressive promenade deck that ran the full length of the steamer. *Westward Ho* was a significant improvement on previous Bristol Channel steamers and gave P. & A. Campbell a boost against the opposition. *Britannia* really sealed Campbell's dominance of Bristol Channel trade. By 1895, its original competitors had ceased business. The company now had a fleet of six steamers and this was further enhanced when the *Glen Rosa* was acquired. The Diamond Jubilee of Queen Victoria in 1897 saw the fortunes of P. & A. Campbell rise even more when it developed South Coast sailings after taking part in the magnificent Fleet Review.

P. & A. Campbell was threatened once again when the Barry Railway Company started paddle steamer services in 1905. This competition quickly became serious and forced P. & A. Campbell to take its opposition to the Barry Railway through the courts, arguing that the Barry Railway was operating services outside its restrictions. A strong legal quarrel went on for two years before the Barry Railway was made to operate within the terms of the Act authorising its foundation. The mighty P. & A. Campbell had triumphed once again. The Edwardian era ended with the Barry fleet being disposed of, some of which were acquired by P. & A. Campbell.

The white-funnelled fleet was further enhanced by the acquisition of more steamers in the years running up to the outbreak of World War 1. This included the *Glen Avon* in 1912 and the *Glen Usk* in 1914. The proud P. & A. Campbell fleet had reached its undoubted heyday, having developed to the point where it could run its operations in the Bristol Channel and on the South Coast perfectly. The larger Campbell steamers were able to undertake excursion work at the height of the season whilst smaller steamers enabled economies to be made when trade was leaner at the start and end of the season.

Although the Campbell fleet looked invincible at the outbreak of World War 1 wartime service meant that after the end of hostilities in 1918 three of the steamers had been lost and three others required far too much work to make them suitable for service, so were withdrawn. The company would never see its pre-war peak return but did still have eight fine paddle steamers left with which to operate Bristol Channel and South Coast services.

*'There were often exciting races on the Cardiff to Weston ferry. On these races Chief Engineer Bill Brown of the* Lady Evelyn

ABOVE *Devonia* (left) and *Brighton Belle* (right) in their heyday. P. & A. Campbell had one of the widest operating areas of any company and provided services at points from the Bristol Channel to the Sussex Coast and to France. Among their greatest adventures were the annual delivery cruises to and from the Bristol Channel to Brighton each summer. *PSPS Collection*

ABOVE Improvements in printing allowed the production of attractive publicity material to entice passengers. Handbills listing cruises by each company from each resort were printed each week. These were normally strung with string through one corner and passengers tore one from the bundle to get information about cruises. *Ron Jones Collection*

*would promise his firemen a flagon of beer if they won the pier and sometimes they got it even if they missed because of their valiant efforts.'* (Bristol Channel, 1919, PSPS Collection)

In 1919 competition came from W. H. Tucker of Cardiff, which placed the *Lady Evelyn* and *Lady Moyra* in service on the Bristol Channel. These steamers had originally operated for the Furness Railway.

*'The* Lady Moyra *used to carry a gilt cock at her masthead which she had had since her Barry Railway days at Gwalia when she had laid claim to the title "Cock of the Channel".'* (Bristol Channel, 1919, PSPS Collection)

**ABOVE** The tradition of going 'Doon the Watter' was an important part of Glasgow life for many decades. The Broomielaw was at the centre of the city and became the principal departure point. Other passengers would board trains for the coast and would then transfer to steamers for the final part of the journey. *PSPS Collection*

**ABOVE** *Duchess of Rothesay* was an elegant member of the Caledonian Steam Packet Company fleet. She was built by J. & G. Thomson of Clydebank and was 225ft long and 26ft wide. Launched on 20 April 1895, she was chiefly employed on the Arran via the Kyles of Bute service from the Upper Firth of Clyde. *PSPS Collection*

**ABOVE** The Glasgow & South Western Railway's *Glen Sannox* in her heyday. She was one of the fastest and most elegant paddle steamers ever built for Firth of Clyde service and the largest railway owned paddle steamer in the UK. She attained a speed of around 20 knots during her trials. *Andrew Gladwell Collection*

**ABOVE** The *Lucy Ashton* was one of the most famous and well-loved paddle steamers of the Firth of Clyde. She was part of the North British Railway fleet and was built by Seath of Rutherglen in 1888. She operated on several routes including Greenock to Helensburgh and Craigendoran to Gareloch, as well as on excursion and relief work. *PSPS Collection*

By 1920 the Campbell fleet had returned to peacetime service and W. H. Tucker went into liquidation in 1922. The 1920s saw a period of calm for the Campbell fleet after what had been over three decades of sometimes fierce competition. P. & A. Campbell took delivery of the splendid new and versatile *Glen Gower* in 1922. It also acquired the *Lady Evelyn* and *Lady Moyra* and renamed them *Brighton Belle* and *Brighton Queen*. With the competition from Tucker out of the way, P. & A. Campbell was once again able to start and reinvigorate its services along the Sussex Coast. The company was now equipped with a fleet that would see no further growth through the 1930s. In 1939 it placed the order for the first turbine steamer in its fleet, to be named *Empress Queen*, but this steamer never appeared due to the outbreak of World War 2. However, like other operators around the rest of the UK, P. &

A. Campbell was planning the introduction of new forms of propulsion that would change the fortunes of paddle steamers.

## Firth of Clyde

The tradition of going 'Doon the Watter' had become a popular feature of Clyde pleasure cruising by the end of Victoria's long reign. As well as the major tourist destinations, the Firth of Clyde also offered a number of smaller calling points. At these a small wooden pier would provide access to a village. A limited amount of holiday accommodation was available but, in the main, these locations were mainly for wealthy businessmen who built impressive villas along the shore at places such as Tighnabruaich.

Firth of Clyde services were dominated by three railway companies: the North British Railway, the Caledonian

265.    "Over The Sea to Skye" from Kyle of Lochalsh.

ARDLUI PIER, LOCH LOMOND.

PIER, KILMUN

**ABOVE** *Duchess of Fife* alongside the pier at Kilmun. Whilst the majority of paddle steamer services on the Firth of Clyde had their final destination at a major resort such as Rothesay or Dunoon, many other services connected with the huge number of remote piers around the Firth. These provided days out for more sedate purposes or for those that lived in remote villages. *PSPS Collection*

**FACING PAGE TOP** David MacBrayne was the principal operator of paddle steamers to the islands and the main calling points away from the Firth of Clyde. The railways later reached Fort William, Kyle of Lochalsh and Mallaig and the steamers linked in with them to provide a fully integrated service. *PSPS Collection*

**FACING PAGE BOTTOM** Services on Loch Lomond developed throughout the heyday of the paddle steamer. The scenic loch provided a wonderful destination for Glaswegians and the best place to view the splendour of places such as Ardlui was from the deck of a paddle steamer. The famous 'Three Lochs Tour' was a particular favourite amongst passengers. *Andrew Gladwell Collection*

Railway and the Glasgow & South Western Railway. The Caledonian Steam Packet Company was formed in 1889 and swiftly ordered a new steamer named the *Caledonia*. She was followed soon after by the *Galatea*. Expansion of rail services followed. This included services to Ardrossan where an important steamer link was provided to Arran by the new *Duchess of Hamilton* in May 1890.

Competition followed and the sight of steamers from rival operators racing on the Clyde became an exciting event. Whilst the Caledonian Steam Packet Company was establishing itself, services elsewhere on the Clyde were also evolving. By the late 1880s *Jeanie Deans* – the North British steamer – was improved to provide greater speed. Further refinements to her passenger accommodation followed.

The Glasgow & South Western Railway started operating its own paddle steamers in 1891. The fleet soon included the *Duchess of Hamilton* and *Glen Sannox*. By 1894 the success of the Glasgow company led to fierce rivalry with the Caledonian company.

The North British company operated from Craigendoran and therefore faced no direct competition from the other companies. Its steamers were some of the greatest of all Clyde steamers, among which were *Lucy Ashton*, *Diana Vernon* and *Guy Mannering*. Its services primarily served Dunoon, Greenock, Arrochar and the main resort of Rothesay.

By the time of Queen Victoria's Diamond Jubilee, the Clyde fleet was at its most magnificent as the rival companies vied with each other by building bigger and better steamers. Inevitably, this had to change and, by the start of Edward VII's reign, steamers such as *Meg Merrilies* were being sold for service elsewhere.

In 1923, the London Midland & Scottish Railway was formed as part of the grouping of the railway companies in Britain into the 'Big Four' companies, and the Caledonian Railway and Glasgow & South Western steamer fleets on the Clyde were amalgamated by the LMS. At the same time, the North British Railway fleet became part of the London &

North Eastern Railway. The other major player on the Clyde, David MacBrayne, continued to offer popular services to more distant destinations from Glasgow and the Firth of Clyde.

The LNER now dominated the north bank services from Craigendoran whilst the LMS dominated services on the south side and along the Ayrshire coast, with a large number of important calling points. This was busy time for Firth of Clyde steamers as steam trains fed the steamers with over four million passengers a year, hungry for a day at the coast. The Broomielaw and Bridge Wharf became the Glasgow steamer embarkation point for Glaswegians during summer months. As they paddled towards the sea, passengers were able to have an excellent view of the countless ships being constructed along the River Clyde. The railway companies were extremely lucky to have such a large market, hungry for trips to the Clyde resorts, whether for the day or an annual holiday. Cheery Glaswegians were famed for their ability to have a good time and they

**ABOVE** The first *Mercury* on the Firth of Clyde. A replacement was built by Fairfield of Govan and launched on 16 January 1934. She became the final paddle steamer delivered to the LMS for its Firth of Clyde fleet but was the first of a new look with enclosed paddle boxes rather than ornamental ones. She entered Clyde service on 4 March 1934 and was transferred to the Caledonian Steam Packet fleet in 1937. *PSPS Collection*

**ABOVE LEFT** The *Princess Patricia* cruising on Loch Lomond. She was one of the former London County Council paddle steamers from the River Thames. *Princess Patricia* had been known as *Shakespeare* on the Thames but was renamed when she was placed in service on Loch Lomond. She operated short excursions as well as winter services on Loch Lomond. She was withdrawn from service in 1938. *PSPS Collection*

**FACING PAGE TOP** The *Queen Mary* was built by Denny of Dumbarton for Williamson-Buchanan. She could carry up to 2,086 passengers, making her the largest excursion steamer in the UK. She operated the hugely popular Glasgow to Rothesay, Millport and Arran run. In 1935 her name changed to *Queen Mary II* when Cunard launched their new liner *Queen Mary*. *Queen Mary II* is shown here towards the end of her career on the Firth of Clyde with her single funnel which replaced the original two funnels. *Andrew Gladwell*

**FACING PAGE BOTTOM** *Talisman* cruising on the Firth of Clyde. She was the first diesel-electric paddle steamer and was built by the famous Inglis yard in 1935. Her diesel engine gave considerable problems throughout her career and she was eventually withdrawn and scrapped during the mid-1960s. *John Gilmore*

**ABOVE** *Juno* was 245 feet in length and was built by Clydebank Engineering & Shipbuilding in 1898. She was launched on 17 June 1898 and provided services from Ayr and Troon. She was scrapped at Alloa in 1932. *Ron Jones*

**ABOVE** The Broomielaw at Glasgow was always a busy place with paddle steamers arriving and departing. Glasgow provided a huge supply of passengers for the steamers, which could reach the Firth of Clyde resorts in a couple of hours. *Andrew Gladwell Collection*

embraced their trip to Rothesay or Dunoon with relish as they escaped their hard lives for a day or two on the elegant steamers of the Clyde with their fine looks, evocative names and beautiful paddle boxes. It was their chance to experience life aboard the steamers that they had proudly built.

As with other areas around the UK, the Clyde had a number of popular resorts in this period. Rothesay on Bute was the undisputed queen and its vast pier was the largest and busiest pier on the Firth of Clyde. As many as 90 arrivals and departures could occur at piers such as Rothesay on a busy summer day. The more scenic cruises and remote destinations such as Tighnabruaich and Inveraray continued to prosper for those wanting a less boisterous destination than Rothesay and there was an intricate network of steamer piers along the Firth of Clyde at this time. These and their steam train connections demonstrated that travel on the Clyde had indeed reached a peak.

The 1920s and 1930s saw Clyde services further enhanced by changes in the fleets. With an established network of routes and piers, the operators were now fully conversant with what was required to maximise profit and usage. Poor routes and inadequate steamers of previous decades had now been dropped. The era was typified by the arrival of some of the most splendid paddle steamers ever to grace the UK's waters.

The LNER was the prime promoter in this new era and the most splendid product of the 1930s was the *Jeanie Deans* of 1931. The LNER steamer was named after the heroine of one of Sir Walter Scott's novels and, with her splendid triple-expansion engine, 18.5-knot speed and beautiful design, she became an immediate hit. She was, at the time of her arrival, the largest paddle steamer to have been built for service at Craigendoran. Her regular route

was on the run to the Ayrshire coast and to Arran, as well as from Craigendoran to Lochgoilhead and Arrochar.

The LMS introduced the *Mercury* and *Caledonia* in 1934. The 1930s was an era of streamlined design and what would have once been ornate and gilded paddle boxes were now built-over so the paddle box was no longer the visual focal point. The *Caledonia* was to become a favourite steamer for many Clyde enthusiasts. Further evolution in design was to follow when the *Talisman* entered service in 1935 for the LNER. She had a conventional decorative vented paddle box and was the first direct-acting diesel-electric paddle steamer to be built. This revolution resulted in economical running but never caught on. *Marchioness of Lorne* was to follow around a year later. She was built for year-round service and provided the important link between small remote piers and the rail-head at Gourock.

The final new paddle steamers to join the Clyde fleets during this period were the *Jupiter* and *Juno*. These were large steamers but sadly lacked ornate paddle boxes. They did, though, possess steam engines, much to the satisfaction of enthusiasts.

The heyday of Clyde steamers also saw a period of prosperity on Loch Lomond. Although lacking the seaside

ABOVE *Glen Sannox* was a fine looking paddle steamer and competed with the *Duchess of Hamilton* on the Isle of Arran route. Like many other large paddle steamers, she was very fast but also burnt a lot of coal. *PSPS Collection*

RIGHT Places such as Greenock, Gourock and Dunoon developed vast piers and embarkation points for the Firth of Clyde paddle steamers. They normally linked in with important railway lines to create a fast and simple way of travelling across the Firth of Clyde. *PSPS Collection*

pleasures of resorts such as Rothesay, the loch instead offered spectacular scenic cruises aboard paddle steamers such as *Princess May* and *Prince Edward*. Steamer services would often link with train and bus services to provide an attractive day trip on the picturesque loch.

The period was also marked by the introduction by attractive new turbine steamers. One of the greatest of these was the *Queen Mary II* built for Williamson-Buchanan in 1933. Further turbine steamers were introduced to replace the ageing *Iona* and *Columba* of the David MacBrayne fleet.

At the end of the 1930s, the Firth of Clyde fleet was still performing well. The decade had seen the introduction of new and revolutionary steamers to replace some of the more elderly Victorian ones and the competition of earlier years had ceased so the many steamers operated amidst an atmosphere of co-operation. Despite the looming prospect of war, the fleets were as popular as ever and were confident of their future.

ABOVE The *Jupiter* was one of the new breed of 1930s paddle steamers that had enclosed paddle boxes instead of decorative vented boxes. They tended to look more like turbine steamers than paddle steamers. *Ron Jones*

ABOVE A rare view of the *Princess Mary* shortly before she was launched. She was built for Red Funnel by Day, Summers & Co. in 1911. She was a versatile steamer built for excursion and tender work and entered service on 17 June 1911. She operated the regular service between Southampton, Cowes and Portsmouth. She was later requisitioned for service during World War 1 and acted as a minesweeper in the Mediterranean before hitting a wreck and sinking. *PSPS Collection*

LEFT *Majestic* was the flagship of the Cosens fleet in the days before World War 1. She undertook trips to France as well as along the Dorset coast. Cosens operated its most extensive routes during the Edwardian period. *Majestic* was lost during the conflict. *Andrew Gladwell Collection*

BELOW *Brighton Queen* was operated by P. & A. Campbell for its expanding Sussex Coast services in 1901. She had a short life undertaking Sussex services before she was sunk during service in World War 1. *Andrew Gladwell Collection*

## South Coast

By the time of Queen Victoria's Diamond Jubilee, the South Coast had a massive fleet. The crowning moment was the Spithead Fleet Review of 1897, the event admirably promoting the attractive features of the South Coast and the lucrative takings that were possible for paddle steamers from other areas. A result of this saw P. & A. Campbell make an entry into South Coast and Southampton services after its steamers *Westward Ho*, *Britannia* and *Cambria* had taken part in the celebrations. In the following year P. & A. Campbell operated *Glen Rosa* and *Cambria* from Southampton. Cruises to Bournemouth, the Isle of Wight and Southsea were also offered, as well as trips to France.

P. & A. Campbell continued to expand its South Coast services but encountered significant competition when Red Funnel and Cosens placed new paddle steamers on services in direct competition. The strongest competition came

**ABOVE** Passengers aboard the *Waverley* on her first trip from Eastbourne in 1911. The P. & A. Campbell services along the Sussex Coast were hugely popular in the years before World War 1. The main departure points were Brighton, Eastbourne and Hastings. Many services were also offered to Deal, Folkestone and Dover in Kent. *PSPS Collection*

from the Southampton-based Red Funnel paddle steamers: *Lorna Doone*, *Bournemouth Queen* and *Balmoral*. Red Funnel had been a prime player on the South Coast for many years and its elegant steamers provided more than adequate opposition to any competitor.

P. & A. Campbell then pushed to expand its services eastwards to serve the huge markets offered by major Sussex resorts of Brighton, Hastings and Eastbourne. It soon realised that Brighton would provide an excellent base. The Sussex Coast had previously only seen modest exploitation of services and P. & A. Campbell purchased the Brighton, Worthing & South Coast Steam Boat Company in 1901. The Palace and West piers provided extensive facilities for visiting paddle steamers and Brighton was reaching its peak as a seaside resort – there were rich pickings to be made especially with the large resorts of Eastbourne and Hastings nearby.

P. & A. Campbell was expanding a hitherto unexploited market with a great deal of potential and which was less of a

battle with other operators. The geographical position of the resorts meant that the company could run services to and from areas such as the Isle of Wight, Southampton, Bournemouth, Southsea, Deal, Margate and Folkestone as well as trips to Boulogne and Cherbourg. The densely printed handbills of the period show the sheer ambition of the company. One of the most exciting and longest cruises of all was the lengthy delivery and return cruises at the start and end of each season from the Bristol Channel to the Sussex Coast.

*'I was at Brighton for Easter 1913 and remember whilst we sailed that two extra lifeboats were being fitted to conform to new regulations following the* Titanic *disaster. On nearing Beachy Head ominous clouds gave warning of an approaching storm and we ran full into it. It was an alarming experience and I wondered whether we would survive it. The little ship stood on end, rocked, jumped and I really feared may sink. Coats, bags and sundry loose articles went overboard with many of the owners too sick to care.'* (South Coast enthusiast, 1913, PSPS Collection)

The Edwardian era on the South Coast was a period of great change as companies adapted to provide a more stable arena of operation. Several steamers were withdrawn because competition was heavy but, although it seemed foolish for other operators to place new large steamers in

**ABOVE** The *Gracie Fields* had one of the shortest careers of any paddle steamer. It was launched by the famous 1930s artiste of the same name who sang her song 'Sing as we Go' as the steamer slid down the slipway. Miss Fields was given a brooch as a gift at the launch with a ruby, pearl, emerald, and sapphire. These were the names of Red Funnel's early steamers! *Andrew Gladwell Collection*

operation on the South Coast, Cosens of Weymouth introduced the popular *Majestic* in 1901. Although long-distance services to France and the Channel Islands were being developed at the time, not all passengers wanted long distance cruises. The Weymouth-based operator Cosens was a very popular and successful operator of paddle steamers and its positioning at the busy seaside resort of Weymouth allowed it to operate services that called at Bournemouth, Swanage, Poole and the Isle of Wight, as well as rarer visits to Torquay or to France. Its most popular cruises were to Portland to view the dockyard or to the picturesque Lulworth Cove where passengers landed direct from the steamer onto the sheltered beach. *Majestic* was followed by *Emperor of India*, which Cosens placed in service in 1906. She had originally been ordered and built by Red Funnel as *Princess Royal*.

In 1908 Red Funnel expanded its excursions services from Bournemouth to enable it to operate to a wide number of places from Torquay in Devon to Eastbourne in Sussex. Both Cosens and Red Funnel spent the final years of the Edwardian era in a battle to gain supremacy of the lucrative Bournemouth trade. The combatants were

**ABOVE** Handbill advertising cruises by Cosen's *Emperor of India* at the Spithead Fleet Review of George VI in 1937. Such rare and special cruises were lucrative for the operating companies who could charge inflated prices for fares, food and liquor. Extra cruises to view the fleet illuminated at night were also promoted. *John Gilmore Collection*

**ABOVE** Crew of the *Lorna Doone*. The deck hands have the Red Funnel abbreviation emblazoned across their jumpers. The company name 'Southampton Isle of Wight & South of England Royal Mail Steam Packet Company Limited' was the longest steamer operating name in the UK and was normally shortened to 'Red Funnel'. *PSPS Collection*

**BELOW** Paddle box of the *Sandown* showing the bland Southern Railway carving at its centre. Paddle steamers normally had elaborate carvings at the centre of the venting which emphasised the character and name of the steamer. *PSPS Collection*

**ABOVE** P. & A. Campbell's *Waverley* at Eastbourne Pier during the heyday of Sussex coast services in Edwardian times. Resorts such as Brighton, Eastbourne and Hastings never became as popular as other areas in the UK and the Sussex coastline had relatively few piers. *John Gilmore.*

**BELOW LEFT** Paddle steamer services from Southsea to Portsmouth were always popular. They were able to link the great ports of Southampton and Portsmouth with the many piers of the Isle of Wights. They also visited placed further afield such as Dorset and Sussex. *Andrew Gladwell Collection*

**BELOW RIGHT** The *Princess Beatrice* arriving at Cowes Pier on the Isle of Wight around 1914. The Isle of Wight became hugely popular in Victorian times due to Queen Victoria's love of the island. Many of the paddle steamers were given royal names as a link to Victoria. *Andrew Gladwell*

Monarch and *Brodick Castle* for Cosens and *Stirling Castle* and *Lord Elgin* for Red Funnel. Further changes took place in the fleets in an effort to gain a supremacy in services (however small). Red Funnel introduced *Princess Mary* and *Princess Helena*. Cosens, on the other hand, sold *Brodick Castle* but introduced the splendid *Alexandra*.

A very impressive 24 paddle steamers were now plying for trade on the South Coast at this time, generating money for all.

*'In those days (1911-13) Brighton Queen carried a man selling fruit, his pitch being just forward of the funnel, and I can recall some pears bought from him near the Nab. The Nab then was a lightship and about half an hour before reaching it the purser came round collecting newspapers etc for the men of the lightship. They were tied up in a bundle and*

**ABOVE** *Princess Elizabeth* was built by Day, Summers & Co for Red Funnel and was launched on 2 June 1927. She was named to commemorate the birth of the young princess who would one day become Elizabeth II. *Princess Elizabeth* operated on a mix of ferry and excursions services from Southampton to the Isle of Wight as well as from Bournemouth. *Andrew Gladwell Collection*

**ABOVE** The engine room of the *Princess Elizabeth*. The Chief Engineer would have this view as he stood on his platform. The large circular dial shows the command from the bridge. The long handles at the bottom controlled the movement of the engine. Passengers always enjoyed seeing the movements of an engine and its cranks and pistons as the steamer approached or departed from a pier. *PSPS Collection*

*Captain West went in very close for it to be thrown aboard. This was a practice with steamers encountering lightships.'* (T. More, PSPS Collection)

*'On a trip round the Isle of Wight on* Brighton Queen *we called at Shanklin and I was surprised at the notice on the pier head "Shanklin Pier Toll Two Pence". They evidently wanted our money more than our visit and I took a dim view of this.'* (E. James, PSPS Collection)

*'Bournemouth (1911-13) was nasty for pier tolls where passengers had to pay on landing and re-embarkation.'* (T. More, PSPS Collection)

After World War 1, South Coast services were reinvigorated by the addition of the *Princess Elizabeth* of 1927. The rise in popularity of outdoor pursuits meant that a steady trickle of passengers now wanted something a little different than a beach-based holiday. The freedom offered by the motor car was also becoming more popular and it was inevitable that the Isle of Wight, as an island, would require Red Funnel to start to accept motor cars long before mainland-based operators. By the mid 1930s Red Funnel was introducing motor vessels such as *Medina* and *Vecta* to its fleet, a trend which was to be followed elsewhere in the UK.

Paddle steamers, however, were still being built for Red Funnel and one of the most exuberant launches in its history took place on 8 April 1936 when Gracie Fields launched the paddle steamer that bore her name. At the time, Gracie Fields was the greatest theatre and recording star in the UK and in her typical jolly style she sang 'Sing As We Go' as the steamer moved down the slipway at the

"QUEEN OF THE NORTH."

**ABOVE** The main shaft of the *Queen of the North* was divided (as with the other Blackpool steamers of that period). The paddle wheels could therefore be operated independently when required. *Queen of the North* is seen here at Blackpool. The letters 'GW' and 'WP' often appeared on Blackpool steamer handbills. The explanation is simple: these letters stood for 'God Willing' or 'Weather Permitting'. *Andrew Gladwell Collection*

**LEFT** Official guide for services offered by the Liverpool & North Wales Steamship Company. The company offered cruises for large numbers of people from Lancashire, Yorkshire, the Midlands and North Wales. Its steamers, such as *La Marguerite*, were some of the largest and most impressive in the UK. *Andrew Gladwell Collection*

launch. Confidence in the future of paddle steamers was at a high and it seemed that services would continue to prosper. The introduction of these newer members of the fleet meant that older steamers could be disposed of and the 1930s was also the decade when faithful old timers such as *Corfe Castle*, *Prince of Wales* and *Princess Beatrice* were scrapped.

In the Coronation year of 1937, Cosens withdrew its elderly paddle steamer *Premier* and replaced her with the *Consul* (ex-*Duke of Devonshire*). *Duchess of Norfolk* was the next to join the fleet and was renamed as *Embassy* by the company.

The need for paddle steamers to operate between the mainland and the Isle of Wight enabled Portsmouth to become a popular embarkation point. The Southern Railway was one of the 'Big Four' railway companies created in 1923. It operated two busy routes to and from the Isle of Wight from the mainland: from Lymington to Yarmouth and Portsmouth to Ryde. Confidence in the 1920s and 1930s resulted in an exciting building programme when no less than seven modern paddle steamers were built for service by the Southern Railway. The South Coast, like the Firth of Clyde and Thames, was following a trend of modernisation. The new steamers – *Shanklin*, *Freshwater*, *Portsdown*, *Southsea*, *Whippingham*, *Sandown* and *Ryde* – were introduced over a period of 13 years. The Southern

Railway had a dual role as both ferry operator and operator of pleasure cruises and the new steamers soon gained popularity and carried out their roles with style.

## North Wales and the North West Coast

Another area that witnessed growth at the end of the Victorian era was North Wales. Being placed amidst some of the most beautiful scenery in the UK and being close to the great cities of the industrial age, the area was perfectly positioned to take full advantage of the paddle steamer.

The Liverpool & North Wales Steamship Company was formed in 1891 and quickly ordered a new ship from Fairfield's yard, which was now a shareholder in the enterprise. The *St Tudno* could carry over 1,000 passengers at a speed of almost 20 knots. She soon settled into her new North Wales life and lasted until 1912, when she was sold for further service elsewhere.

*St Tudno* was joined by the *St Elvies* in 1896. She was another product of the Fairfield yard and was a splendid-looking steamer. She wasn't quite as large as her sister but had the added advantage of consuming less coal than the coal-hungry *St Tudno*.

An absorption of another shipping company followed in 1899 when the Snowdon Passenger Steamship Company was acquired by the Liverpool & North Wales Steamship Company. It now had the charming paddle steamer

**ABOVE** *Greyhound* arriving at Heysham. She had excellent passenger accommodation. This included a dining saloon, two private staterooms, smoking room, bar, ladies' room as well as ample lavatories. To the bow were second class areas with space set aside for dancing to the extent of four sets. Below this was a second class dining saloon. The promenade deck was 217ft in length and had ample teak seating. Music on each cruise was provided by a trio of musicians. *Andrew Gladwell Collection*

**BELOW** After the disappointment of the *Philomel*, the Furness Railway purchased the Bristol Channel paddle steamer *Gwalia*. She could easily make the Fleetwood to Barrow run in 45 minutes if required and could accommodate 1,015 passengers. She left Barry on 11 May 1910 and her name was changed from *Gwalia* to *Lady Moyra* on 26 May 1910. *Andrew Gladwell Collection*

ABOVE *Belle* was originally built for the Llandudno & Caernarfon Steamboat Company Limited. After initial service in North Wales, she transferred to the Southport to Blackpool run. She was an attractive vessel with a white hull and heavily gilded paddle box. She ran to Southport nearly every day as well as offering short sea cruises to Morecambe Bay from Blackpool North Pier. *Andrew Gladwell Collection*

*Snowdon* at its disposal, which was a great deal smaller than *St Tudno* and *St Elvies*. Such amalgamations often meant that larger paddle steamers became the main vessels with smaller steamers such as the *Snowdon* working on 'feeder' services from the main calling points. North Wales was an excellent example of this as the large steamers would convey passengers from Liverpool to the most prominent North Wales pier at Llandudno whilst smaller steamers would then take passengers to the more restricted scenic beauties of the Menai Straits.

When *La Marguerite* arrived in North Wales in 1904, she joined a regional fleet that was flourishing. She couldn't have been more different to the smaller *Snowdon*, able to carry 2,077 passengers against the 462 of the *Snowdon*. Liverpool, with its proximity to the great industrial conurbations of the North West, offered a splendid platform from which the Liverpool & North Wales Steamship Company could operate paddle steamers and despite having a fairly large fleet, the North Wales company continued to expand as it flourished in the Edwardian era. It acquired two more new vessels – *St Trillo* and *St Elian* – to give it an impressive fleet of six paddle steamers.

The Liverpool & North Wales Steamship Company was one of the first to replace paddle steamers with turbine steamers. In 1925 *La Marguerite* was withdrawn and the company chose a turbine steamer to replace her. Although visually a world away from *La Marguerite* and other paddle steamers, turbine steamers such as her

replacement the *St Tudno* could comfortably carry up to 2,493 passengers at a speed of up to 19 knots. The older paddle steamers were gradually replaced by the smart new turbine steamers during the 1920s and 1930s but although the scene was set for these new vessels to dominate services, war interrupted day cruises to the North Wales coast once again.

Another cruising area close to North Wales was the Lancashire coast and in particular the vast seaside resorts of Blackpool and Southport. The mid 1890s were very much the heyday of paddle steamers from the two resorts. The introduction of the handsome *Greyhound* in 1895, operated by the North Pier Steamship Company, represented a new level of style and service along the Lancashire coast but the final few years of the 19th and first few years of the 20th century saw troubled years for the steamers. From 1895 onwards, competition was becoming intense and large steamers began to offer similar services to the same destinations, thereby creating a position that couldn't be sustained. Steamer business was also heavily dependent on the Lancashire cotton

**ABOVE** *Queen of the North* between the Central and North piers at Blackpool. Despite being the UK's most popular resort, Blackpool was never able to sustain a long-life as a paddle steamer resort. Weather, silting and the massive number of amusements in the town ensured that passengers remained on land.
*Andrew Gladwell Collection*

**ABOVE** Lancashire newspapers were often full of negative stories detailing adventures at sea. In 1901, around 250 passengers boarded the *Clifton* at Blackpool. After half an hour, the advertised cruise to Morecambe Bay was cancelled, and according to reports passengers 'suffered' for five hours as attempts were made to get the steamer alongside the pier. Passengers were said to have been 'terrified' and many collapsed in a 'dead swoon'. *Andrew Gladwell Collection*

**BELOW** *Bickerstaffe* operated from Blackpool Central Pier and was owned by Sir John Bickerstaffe who built Blackpool Tower. This steamer operated cruises to Southport, North Wales and the Isle of Man. *Andrew Gladwell Collection*

industry. Economic slumps, such as that in the early years of the 20th century, had a significant effect on steamer trade. The shifting sands along the Lancashire coast also meant that jetties soon became virtually inaccessible, or access for steamers was limited to just a few hours a day. The result was that most pier companies had to embark on large projects to extend their jetties to allow access at all states of the tide. This was expensive and, combined with the introduction of new vessels such as the North Pier's *Deerhound*, the burden became too much and amalgamations became a feature of the Lancashire coast steamer business. The once great North Pier Steamship Company of Blackpool was one such casualty, being absorbed by the rival Blackpool Passenger Steamboat Company in 1905.

The period from 1900 to 1914 saw one particularly popular paddle steamer service maintain its business – the Furness Railway's service from Fleetwood to Barrow. The enterprising General Manager Alfred Aslett introduced the ultimate day excursion that transported the holiday masses from Blackpool by train to Fleetwood and then across Morecambe Bay by large steamers such as *Lady Moyra* or *Lady Evelyn* for onward journeys by train, carriage and lake steamer to enjoy the breathtaking and unrivalled scenic beauty of the Lake District for just a few shillings. But even this delightful service was short lived, being cruelly terminated by World War 1.

The boom experienced in other areas of the UK during the decades after World War 1 was never replicated at Blackpool and Southport. Blackpool, despite being the UK's most popular seaside resort, never experienced a period of prosperity for pleasure steamer services during

the 1920s and 1930s. The availability of fast and cheap train services plus the ever-increasing reliance on the charabanc provided the resort with a more than adequate number of visitors. The town also had such a wide number of palaces of pleasure that there was no need to go on a pleasure cruise. After service during World War 1, *Greyhound* returned to Blackpool but was sold in April 1923 for further service at Belfast. *Bickerstaffe* of the Central Pier remained at Blackpool during the 1920s but was withdrawn in 1928. This ended regular service from Blackpool and it was left to steamers such as *Snowdon*, *Minden* and *Queen of the Bay* to offer short-lived and irregular services from the North Pier in the years that followed.

# 3

# Ferries and Paddle Steamers in Rivers and Estuaries

**ABOVE** *Gordon* on the Thames at Woolwich on 2 December 1962. The old Woolwich paddle ferries performed an incredibly important job in the days before the tunnels and the bridge were built at Dartford. They conveyed a large number of vehicles and passengers reliably across the short distance of the river each day. Paddle steamers performed an important role as ferries around the UK. *PSPS Collection*

**ABOVE** *Hotspur* was the Hythe ferry from 1889 until 1927. She was quite small, at 80ft in length, and could carry up to 200 passengers. She was later renamed *G.E.C.* and after withdrawal had her engine and anything of value removed. She was then allowed to rot at Dibden Bay. *Andrew Gladwell*

It would be easy to assume that the use of paddle steamers was confined to excursions around the coastline of the UK, but they also saw usage at many ports and harbours as paddle tugs, as well as in smaller rivers, lakes and estuaries as ferries and working craft.

Paddle steamers that served the large seaside resorts inevitably stole the limelight as the most popular and recognisable of their ilk, but there were many other fleets of paddle steamers around the UK that developed services to serve their local area more modestly. These often became highly distinctive in their design, built by local shipbuilders to conform with the geography and navigation needs of the waterway. Every feature was designed or evolved to enable the steamer to arrive and depart with the minimum of effort and to carry out its work without delay. They often had a primary use for ferrying people or goods or assisting other vessels, and only later developed into becoming a part of the tourism industry. They were not luxurious or large, but were instead comfortable and practical. They might also have a dual role for locals who used them to travel to and from local towns or to market. These steamers were not usually sea-going vessels and therefore their design could

**LEFT** The River Dart steamers evolved to operate a near-perfect paddle steamer service on the picturesque Devon river. This Edwardian view shows the charming design and simple layout of the steamers of the time, which was similar to that of the later *Kingswear Castle*, built in 1924. Note the large numbers of passengers aboard the steamer. *PSPS Collection*

**ABOVE** The Woolwich ferry *Hutton* provided an important down-river link across the River Thames. The ferry has always been free and for the impoverished it provided a free day out as they cruised backwards and forwards across the river. For many, it was the equivalent of a day at the seaside. *Andrew Gladwell Collection*

**FACING PAGE TOP** Many paddle steamers had dual roles as tugs and for excursions. *Queen* was part of the Cosens fleet and operated from Weymouth. Cosens had the lucrative contract for ferrying sailors to and from the nearby Portland Dockyard. *Andrew Gladwell Collection/*

**FACING PAGE BOTTOM** The *Prince Edward* at Saltash in September 1927. Many paddle steamers led busy lives working on rivers and transporting local people and tourists for all of their lives. These steamer services are now almost forgotten at many locations. *Andrew Gladwell Collection*

**ABOVE** The paddle ferries at Woolwich on the Thames were perhaps some of the hardest working paddle steamers ever to operate. A steam ferry service was first operated in 1889. The first ferries were side-loading paddle steamers and were named *Gordon*, *Duncan* and *Hutton*. The paddle steamers were replaced by the present fleet in 1963. *John Gilmore*

be more compact and more distinct as they did not need the power, passenger facilities or coal capacity of their sea-going sisters.

The earliest of these steamers around the rivers of the UK during the early and mid-Victorian period were similar to each other. Within a decade or two, operators became aware of the particular needs of the goods they carried and their passengers. Towards the late Victorian era, larger and more distinct designs of paddle steamers were emerging around the country.

As developments were made in other forms of transport, the use of paddle steamers for transporting goods and livestock, as well as for ferry services, diminished and inevitably in some areas the services ceased. The growth of a comprehensive railway network, the building of bridges across rivers and estuaries and the creation of better roads provided an easier means of transporting goods than the paddle steamer, which was reliant on the weather or tides. It was a natural progression, therefore, for the paddle steamer that once provided an important trade or ferry link to adapt to carry holidaymakers. In some areas, such as on the River

**ABOVE** Paddle tugs were generally small and spent long careers in one area. In the North East paddle tugs continued on the River Tyne until the 1950s, as this line up at South Shields in July 1954 shows. *Andrew Gladwell Collection*

**LEFT** *Lord Nelson* departing from Great Yarmouth. The town marked the most northerly destination that could be reached from London by short excursions. *Lord Nelson* was a steam tug and offered relatively short trips from the resort. *Andrew Gladwell Collection*

Humber, paddle ferry services survived until as late as the 1970s but with the building of structures such as the Humber Bridge even the long-lived services eventually ceased.

## Paddle Tugs

The life of the paddle tug was very much overshadowed by the harnessing of paddle power to excursion steamers. The coastal excursion steamers were ornately decorated vessels that plied between seaside piers carrying holidaymakers. The paddle tug lacked this aura, being the unsung hero of many ports and harbours around the UK.

The paddle tug emerged with the construction of the *Charlotte Dundas* on the Forth and Clyde Canal in Scotland in 1803. This new means of towing and manoeuvring ships was highly successful due to the increase in speed in handling that it offered. Inevitably, more paddle tugs were introduced and, shortly afterwards, there were fourteen operating on the

River Tyne alone. The success on the Tyne was soon copied at other ports including Liverpool, Hull and Sunderland. London welcomed its first paddle tug in 1832 when the *Lady Dundas* entered service. One of the most prominent of Thames towage companies started when John Watkins introduced the *Monarch* in 1833. She was later painted by Turner in his popular work 'The Fighting Temeraire'.

The early tugs were built of wood. A common problem was that their working area was limited by the amount of coal that they could carry. By the middle of the 19th century, the Watkins company had greatly expanded its fleet and had also developed the design to enable paddle tugs to work over longer distances. Tugs were no longer restricted to working within short distances but could now tow as far as France. By 1866 Watkins had built its most famous paddle tug, named the *Anglia*. She was simply the most powerful tug to have been built at that date. One of her most notable roles was to transport 'Cleopatra's Needle' to London.

The design of the paddle tug had not changed significantly for over 30 years, although there had been some changes,

**ABOVE** *Eppleton Hall* was a paddle tug built in 1914 mainly to tow large coal-carrying ships at the Tyne Dock at Newcastle-upon-Tyne. After a career on the Tyne, she was withdrawn and was finally relocated to San Francisco in 1970 for her preservation. *Andrew Gladwell*

**BELOW** The paddle tug *Reliant* at Seaham in 1967. *Reliant* was later dismantled and became the central exhibit in the Neptune Hall at the National Maritime Museum at Greenwich. Visitors were able to walk in and around the steamer to appreciate the layout and look of a paddle tug. *Andrew Gladwell*

including the fitting of two boilers on board, but by the 1870s a new development occurred when paddle tugs with disconnected paddle wheels became more common. This allowed separate engines to operate each wheel independently, so that they could move in different directions, making the tug much more manoeuvrable. After this, however, there was little that could be developed further in the paddle tug and it remained virtually the same until screw-power replaced it. The paddle tug had no need to become larger or more luxurious, unlike the excursion paddle steamer, and so it was only the advent of the screw propeller with its greater fuel economy, increased power and low maintenance costs that signalled the end for the paddle tug. It did, though, remain in various isolated roles and areas.

Paddle tugs had a long career with the Royal Navy as they were ideal for working in the confined and very busy environments of the docks. Many of these had remarkably long and hardworking careers, such as the *Sprite*, built in 1915 by Thornycroft and scrapped in 1960. The *Pert* was the last steam paddle tug owned by the Admiralty as well as being the largest. At over 178ft in length, *Pert* had entered service in 1916. She could attain a speed of over 12 knots and had 17 auxiliary steam engines and three boilers. Her power was immense and she could tow the aircraft carrier *Ark Royal* or three destroyers single-handedly. In the late 1950s the Admiralty recognised the important role of paddle tugs and built an impressive fleet of replacement diesel-electric paddle tugs to replace the older steam ones.

Paddle tugs continued for several more decades in the North East of England at places such as Middlesbrough, Sunderland and Seaham, due to the abundance of cheap and plentiful supplies of coal. Even in the early 1960s four steam paddle tugs remained at North East ports. *Roker* was based at Methil and dated back to 1904, when she was built for service on the Wear. *Eppleton Hall* was built in 1914 mainly to tow large coal-carrying ships at the Tyne Dock at Newcastle-upon-Tyne. *The John H. Amos* was based at Middlesbrough and had been built in 1931 for the Tees Conservancy Commissioners for a cost of £18,500. As well as her port work, she was able to carry up to 144 passengers on cruises with a crew of six – a master, mate, two engineers, a stoker and a deck hand. *Old Trafford* was built at South Shields in 1907 for use on the Manchester Ship Canal. She worked hard on the canal until 1950, when she was acquired for further service at Newcastle before moving to Seaham in 1956 and renamed as *Reliant*. She soldiered on in service until 1967.

## River Dart

The River Dart in Devon developed a fleet of distinctive paddle steamers that were built specifically for the river. The first paddle steamer to ply the River Dart was the *Dart* of 1836. Thereafter, little changed on the river until the 1856-built *Dartmouth* entered service. For the next few decades, various small paddle steamers operated on the river and in 1879 one of the first major paddle steamers on the Dart – the *Berry Castle* – entered service and set the

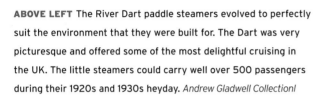

**ABOVE LEFT** The River Dart paddle steamers evolved to perfectly suit the environment that they were built for. The Dart was very picturesque and offered some of the most delightful cruising in the UK. The little steamers could carry well over 500 passengers during their 1920s and 1930s heyday. *Andrew Gladwell Collectionl*

**TOP RIGHT** The first *Kingswear Castle* was built in 1904. She worked on the Dart until a replacement steamer entered service in 1924. The engine from the steamer shown here was removed and placed on the new steamer. Other fixtures were also removed and placed on the new *Kingswear Castle*. *Andrew Gladwell Collection*

**BELOW** The River Dart steamers were hugely popular during the 1920s and 1930s. Their decks always seemed to be full of passengers as they plied between Dartmouth and Totnes. Here, the *Kingswear Castle* crosses the mouth of the Dart early in her career. *Andrew Gladwell Collection*

**ABOVE** Paddle steamer services were developed on the River Dart from the 1830s onwards. Primarily they linked Dartmouth with Totnes but later developments saw places such as Dittisham and Sharpness gain piers to provide a transport link. *Andrew Gladwell Collection*

ABOVE The Dart at Kingswear was wide as it was close to the mouth of the river. Conditions were very different at Totnes and the steamers had to be designed to ensure they were able to turn there.
*Andrew Gladwell Collection*

style for all further steamers that would ply on the river. She was joined by the *Dartmouth Castle* in 1885 and the *Totnes Castle* in 1894. At the start of the next century, in 1904, the first *Kingswear Castle* was built for service between Dartmouth and Totnes. She was built by Cox & Co of Falmouth, as were her engines. These engines survive today in the second paddle steamer that bears the name.

Early steamers were often used for transporting goods and people to market or local towns. This was an era when the weekly market was important to the communities that lined a river. People did not move far from their homes and the geographical isolation of places such as Totnes meant that the early paddle steamers were a vital means of visiting the local town or village to sell their goods, to buy items from a market or to visit people. However, with the growth of tourism, it was natural that the beauty of places such as the River Dart would eventually be exploited as local businesses on the Dart saw the opportunity for making money out of trippers, much as those at the major seaside resorts that were expanding at the time.

Paddle steamers on the Dart had by this time evolved to a more or less uniform style. Built by local builders, each steamer had a single and wide main deck without any deck houses apart from a wheelhouse or raised platform for the master to navigate the steamer. Below this deck were small saloons that were basic in appearance but provided cover in inclement weather. These saloons were accessed by unique well decks placed close to the waterline at the bow and the stern. In order to land passengers at all states of the tide, flying bridges were later added to the main deck to give access to the raised area by steps. The length of each steamer was limited by the width of the river at places such as Totnes. The steamers had to turn by means of ropes and the length of each steamer could not be greater than the width of the river.

In 1914, a new steamer named *Compton Castle* was built. She had smaller porthole-style windows instead of the previous large square ones, as well as a decked sponson. Services continued during World War 1 and although the company had started to introduce motor vessels by the early 1920s, the love of traditional paddle steamers was confirmed when a new *Totnes Castle* and *Kingswear Castle* were built and introduced for Dart service in 1924. Both steamers bore great similarities to those that they replaced. They were very obviously built for the Dart and designed to ensure that passengers were conveyed in great numbers at all states of the tide and to all locations. With their two saloons and ample open deck, both steamers could each impressively hold over 500 passengers at busy periods. They later had flying bridges fitted to aid landing at Dartmouth and Totnes in poor tidal conditions. They were also noteworthy in that many of the old fittings, wood panelling and brasswork were removed from the earlier steamers that bore their names and refitted, as well as the engine of the first *Kingswear Castle*.

Services on the River Dart peaked in the 1920s and 1930s. This was a time of mass tourism when many people were able to sample a holiday for the first time. The picturesque Dart was perfect for trippers from nearby Torquay and the *Kingswear Castle, Totnes Castle, Compton*

ABOVE *Totnes Castle* at Totnes around the time when she entered service in 1924. She was built by Philip & Son of Dartmouth and her design meant that she drew only three feet of water which ideally suited the shallow River Dart. Her popularity during the 1920s was due as much to the modest fare of one shilling and sixpence for a single trip. Motor cycles were also carried for three shillings as long as their tanks were empty. *Andrew Gladwell Collection*

ABOVE Paddle steamers are most widely remembered for providing services to and from large seaside piers but these piers required large steamers and crews to match. It is less often remembered that small rivers and estuaries developed services to enable smaller steamers with just a few crew members to link remote villages such as Duncannon shown here as well as to provide tourist services. *Andrew Gladwell Collection*

*Castle* and *Dartmouth Castle* were as important a part of the scenery as the villages and towns that lined the riverbanks. Railway companies such as the Great Western Railway operated huge publicity machines that vigorously promoted connecting steam train services to the River Dart. Large paddle steamers such as the *Duchess of Devonshire* and *Duke of Devonshire* connected with the Dart from the sea from resorts further afield. Charabanc passengers were also enticed into taking a land and sea cruise to admire the outstanding scenery of Devon. Inevitably, such a boom was followed by change on the outbreak of World War 2 in 1939. Services became very limited during the war and steamers undertook wartime ferry service. Although services resumed as normal with peace, in the years after the war the fleet was modernised with motor vessels. By the early 1960s the elderly paddle steamers required extensive repairs to equip them for further service and directors decided to replace them with new tonnage. *Compton Castle* was first to go and was followed soon after by *Totnes Castle*. The last, *Kingswear Castle*, survived a little longer as she had undergone major repairs in 1961 but by 1965 poor weather and age made her uneconomic to run and she was withdrawn from service, thereby ending a paddle steamer tradition on the River Dart that had lasted well over a century. However, after a lengthy restoration and period of successful operation on

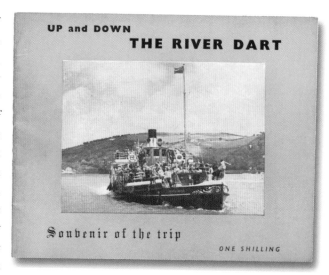

UP and DOWN
**THE RIVER DART**

Souvenir of the trip

ONE SHILLING

ABOVE Although commentaries were often given on many pleasure steamers, passengers often purchased a small guide to give them information on the sights seen during the cruise. The guides not only improved the cruise but also gave some ideas on what to do when passengers reached their destination. *Andrew Gladwell Collection*

RIGHT The *Duke of Devonshire* and *Duchess of Devonshire* provided a popular service in Devon during the post-World War 1 period. They were able to link many resorts and beaches that would have been difficult to reach by train or road. *PSPS Collection*

*Kingswear Castle* on the River Dart in June 2013. This steamer operated on the River Dart from 1924 until 1965 when she was purchased and restored by dedicated volunteers of the Paddle Steamer Preservation Society on the River Medway. She relocated to the River Dart in December 2012. *Chris Jones*

**ABOVE** Dartmouth provided a wonderful backdrop for the delightful little paddle steamers on the River Dart but by the 1960s, the distinctive paddlers were being withdrawn, to be replaced by modern, economic motor vessels that lacked the special features of their predecessors. By the mid-1960s, the paddle steamer fleet had gone. *Andrew Gladwell Collection*

**BELOW** *Wingfield Castle* on the Humber in October 1967. She was built by William Gray & Company at Hartlepool for the LNER and launched in 1934. She operated the Humber service from Hull to New Holland and also undertook trips to Grimsby, Immingham and Reads Island. *PSPS Collection*

the River Medway in Kent, *Kingswear Castle* returned to the River Dart in December 2012.

## River Humber

The River Humber also developed a distinctive fleet of paddle steamers over the years to cope with the very wide estuary that was linked to the North Sea with strong tides (and a tendency to silt up). Although only operating in the river or estuary, the steamers were strongly built like sea-going paddle steamers.

Services were operated principally between Gainsborough, Goole, Hull and Grimsby. Sometimes, linking calls were made to small settlements such as Barton, Burton upon Stather and Ferriby. Such calls provided a vital link to these isolated communities and enabled people to transport their livestock as well as goods to market. The carrying of cattle and sheep was an important part of the business of these steamers.

Paddle steamer services started on the Humber as far back as 1814 when services linked Hull with Selby and Gainsborough. The ferry service linking Lincolnshire and

**ABOVE** Passengers aboard the *Wingfield Castle* during the 1960s. She was a big steamer and could carry up to 16 cars and 1,200 passengers, with two saloons on her main deck and another on her lower deck. She was withdrawn from service on the Humber in 1974 for static use. *PSPS Collection*

Yorkshire was inaugurated in 1820. With the arrival of the railways, services were soon offered by the railway companies from 1845 onwards. By 1923, the London & North Eastern Railway operated the link and introduced *Tattershall Castle* and *Wingfield Castle* in 1934. The success of these paddle steamers was due especially to the fact that they had wide open car decks at their stern and the final steamer which entered service, *Lincoln Castle*, was also built to carry cars across the Humber. However, although they could meet the demand to carry vehicles for a while, the increase in car usage meant they eventually became too small to keep up with this demand. When the Humber Bridge was finally opened in 1981 it signalled the end of the Humber paddle steamer services.

*Wingfield Castle* at Hull Corporation Pier in October 1967. The River Humber saw paddle steamer services thrive for more than a century. The final paddle steamer fleet of *Lincoln Castle*, *Tattershall Castle* and *Wingfield Castle* are fondly remembered and the vessels have generally had long preservation lives. *Eric Jones*

# 4

# Life aboard
# the Steamers

**ABOVE** Passengers sitting in an orderly manner aboard the *Duchess of
Devonshire* during the 1920s. She operated along the South Devon coast for most
of her career until she was beached and wrecked at Sidmouth in August 1934
whilst landing passengers on the beach. *PSPS Collection*

Many steamers operated for around five months a year and so they had to earn as much as possible to pay the costs of summer operation as well as refits during the winter months when they were not in service.

Paddle steamers originally had a spartan look to their layout and facilities and a cruise in the early days lacked the comfort and style of that of later years. From the 1890s onwards they required a great deal of stores such as meat, cakes, beers, wine and ice cream when running their services. As much as eight tons of stores had to be loaded aboard by hand in the hours before the steamer sailed and as soon as the paddle steamer returned from the cruise, work began immediately to clean

and prepare for the next day. Most paddle steamers were coal-fired in the early days and the coal also had to be loaded aboard the steamer ready for the following day.

Working aboard a pleasure steamer was usually very hard work. As many as 60 stewards and cooks might work in a large catering department and others were employed as

BELOW *Balmoral* at Bournemouth. When paddle steamers called at seaside resorts it was a busy time for officers and crew as the vessel was moored and tickets were checked. *Balmoral* entered service in 1900 to compete with the *Cambria* and often cruised to France. *PSPS Collection*

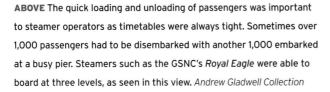

ABOVE The quick loading and unloading of passengers was important to steamer operators as timetables were always tight. Sometimes over 1,000 passengers had to be disembarked with another 1,000 embarked at a busy pier. Steamers such as the GSNC's *Royal Eagle* were able to board at three levels, as seen in this view. *Andrew Gladwell Collection*

ABOVE The 'Mahogany' private dining saloon on the *Royal Eagle*. Large steamers such as this were able to provide luxurious private rooms for the use of parties. These could accommodate between 12 and 50 passengers at a modest extra charge.
*Andrew Gladwell Collection*

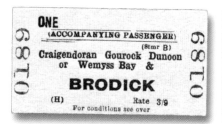

**RIGHT** The purser was one of the busiest crew members. He issued a large number of coloured tickets as well as checking them on disembarkation. Usually, he would have a large rack with these tickets in his office. Each colour of ticket was linked to a different destination and fare type. *Andrew Gladwell Collection*

**ABOVE** Catering departments on paddle steamers were very busy. Patrons dined in style and large numbers could be served. Tickets were issued for each sitting. In the early days, a steward would walk around the decks ringing a hand bell to signal a particular sitting of a meal. *Andrew Gladwell Collection*

**LEFT** Companies such as P. & A. Campbell issued special season tickets and coupons to their most enthusiastic customers. *PSPS Collection*

**FACING PAGE TOP** The arrival or departure of a paddle steamer was always an exciting thing to watch. Here, *Cambria* is seen here alongside at Ilfracombe with passengers aboard waiting to depart on a cruise and others queuing for steamers. Missing a steamer at places such as this in the Bristol Channel or elsewhere could mean a long and difficult journey home by other means. *PSPS Collection*

**FACING PAGE BOTTOM** A busy deck view of *City of Rochester* on the River Medway taken in 1911. Pre-World War 1 paddle steamers always seemed to be full. She had an open fore deck with a bridge forward of her funnel and could carry up to 1,000 passengers. She served as a tender during World War 1. *Andrew Gladwell Collection*

officers, pursers and deckhands. Some of the largest paddle steamers had up to 100 crew and even on smaller ones the crew could number around 40.

'The masters in this period wore frock coats and carried two rings, with a curl, similar to a naval lieutenant. Two captains took over Royal Sovereign and Koh-i-Noor in 1909 and wore short jackets, creating a precedent. The frock coats disappeared with the period.' (Edward Smith, PSPS Collection)

'In those days, crew replacements were easily come by for there was usually somebody always waiting for a job. This applied even to stokers. One of the features of the Royal Sovereign and Koh-i-Noor was the habit of stokers who banged their shovels against the ventilator for passengers "not to forget" the black-squad below. Many copper coins were thrown down the shaft as a response!' (Edward Smith, PSPS Collection)

'The lavatory attendant did well, and although they only paid a nominal sum, was reputed to be the richest man on the ship. He would stand at the door of his spotless toilets, immaculately dressed, shaking his copper coins – nearly everybody added a penny to his collection and he did a twelve hour day with 1,500 passengers aboard!' (Edward Smith, PSPS Collection)

'Shortly before the 1909 season I heard of a clerk being required in the office of New Palace Steamers. I was in my element. The congenial work was concerned chiefly with purser duties and bookstall work although the hours were awkward and long including long and arduous Sunday work. I had to make many visits to the ships and sometimes, at busy periods, assisted the purser on board. Sometimes I would leave the office in early afternoon and travel to Southend by train to pick up the Koh-i-Noor to check the bookstall on the way up to Tilbury. The railway company was lavish with its season tickets to personnel of the New Palace Steamers and although issued with a third class ticket I could usually get a first class one. Once on the 'Kohy' I would finish my work as quickly as possible to enjoy the rest of the trip and have a first class meal, both ships being renowned for their catering.' (Edward Smith, PSPS Collection)

The day on board would start for most passengers around 30 minutes before the steamer departed. On some of the larger steamers over 2,300 passengers could be accommodated. This was, of course, a major operation that had to be conducted in a very short space of time. Even on smaller steamers it was common for 500-800 passengers to be carried.

**ABOVE** The dining saloon of the *Medway Queen*. Refreshment facilities aboard smaller steamers were more modest than those on larger steamers. Meals were often traditional with roast beef, fried fish and meat salads being particular favourites. Cooking was usually done on a coal stove. *PSPS Collection*

**RIGHT** Catering was always important on pleasure steamers. Tickets were normally issued for dining in the restaurants and patrons had to book a particular time to eat. They had to depart swiftly for the next diners to enjoy their meal. This Eagle & Queen Line menu from 1938 shows some of the options for breakfast. *PSPS Collection*

**FACING PAGE TOP** Passengers disembarking from a paddle steamer at Ilfracombe during the 1920s. In this view you can see one of the lifeboats as well as the buoyant seats with grab ropes behind the queue. The *Titanic* disaster of 1912 resulted in paddle steamers improving their lifesaving equipment. *PSPS Collection*

**FACING PAGE BOTTOM** Prosperous looking passengers aboard a General Steam Navigation paddle steamer on the Thames during the 1920s. The steamers allowed middle and working class passengers to travel together in what was a class conscious age. Naturally, though, they were kept apart in separate parts of the ship. *Andrew Gladwell Collection*

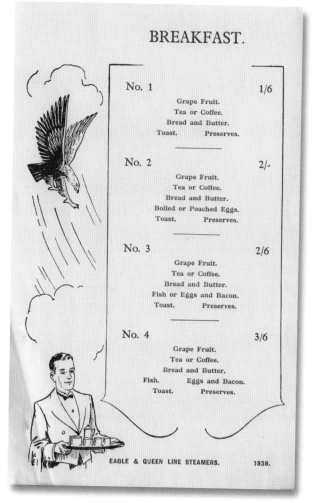

**BREAKFAST.**

No. 1                                          1/6
Grape Fruit.
Tea or Coffee.
Bread and Butter.
Toast.          Preserves.

No. 2                                          2/-
Grape Fruit.
Tea or Coffee.
Bread and Butter.
Boiled or Poached Eggs.
Toast.          Preserves.

No. 3                                          2/6
Grape Fruit.
Tea or Coffee.
Bread and Butter.
Fish or Eggs and Bacon.
Toast.          Preserves.

No. 4                                          3/6
Grape Fruit.
Tea or Coffee.
Bread and Butter.
Fish.          Eggs and Bacon.
Toast.          Preserves.

EAGLE & QUEEN LINE STEAMERS.          1938.

**ABOVE** The officers and crew of the *Woolwich Belle* in 1891 soon after the steamer had entered service. She was one of the smallest of the Belle fleet and when built was fitted with a telescopic mast. She spent a lot of her Belle career at Ipswich and Great Yarmouth. *PSPS Collection*

*'There was an unfortunate incident in 1920 when the company was fined £40 for carrying 25 passengers over the number on* Lady Moyra *making a return trip from Ilfracombe. It was difficult to be sure of the totals aboard when the crowds were pushing to embark and, on a good day, at Weston more people sometimes waited for the last boat than could lawfully be carried – yet it was hardly a human gesture to leave them behind. On one occasion,* Lady Evelyn *was possibly 'tipping the scales' and the officials were awaiting her arrival at Cardiff. While they prepared to check and re-check the passengers descending by the main gangway, another gangway was slipped out from the other side of the ship onto the deck of another steamer. Hastily a crowd of passengers was hustled across the ship's deck and ashore onto a different pontoon.'* (Bristol Channel, 1920, PSPS Collection)

Once aboard, passengers could choose to upgrade to get a deckchair or have a seat in a sun lounge on the payment of a small fee. Once the cruise was underway, passengers would buy their tickets from the purser to enjoy the many facilities on offer. A lot of men went to 'see the engine', which meant that they would visit the bar that was normally positioned close to the engine! The gleaming polished engine was also usually on view to the passengers through an open panel and the opportunity to observe the engine in action was a unique attraction of pleasure steamers.

*'The engines contribute to a paddle steamer's "atmosphere" and one could watch them for hours without getting bored.'* (Tom Bradley, PSPS Collection)

*'An interesting tradition on the New Palace steamers was the ringing of the ship's bell to mark the passage of time every half*

**ABOVE** Several operating companies offered day trips to France from South Coast and Thames resorts. These became incredibly popular and allowed passengers a few hours ashore in France before returning to the UK. For most Victorian and Edwardian passengers the experience of spending time in a different country was a novel one. *Andrew Gladwell Collection*

**RIGHT** A day out on a paddle steamer was for many a once-a-year experience. Passengers aboard paddle steamers such as the *Duke of Devonshire* or *Duchess of Devonshire* could enjoy the glorious Devon scenery from their deckchair. *PSPS Collection*

**BELOW RIGHT** In the days before internet tickets, the purser would normally have vast stocks of different coloured tickets that would indicate the destination visited and type of ticket. These were held in racks in his office. *Andrew Gladwell Collection*

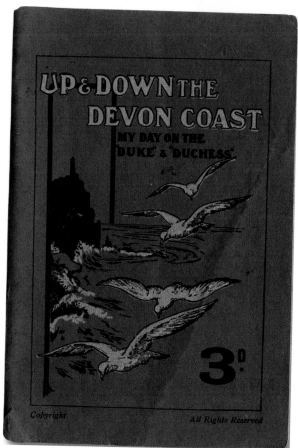

*hour throughout the day.'* (Edward Smith, PSPS Collection)

Meals were usually arranged at timed sittings and a ticket was obtained for a particular slot. Dining was organised in military style by the chief steward and patrons had to finish their meal within the allotted time before the next diners were ushered in. Often a bell was rung to signal service. It was usual for waiters to be dressed in smart uniforms and food was often served on crested china and silver-plate. Dining was something to be enjoyed and was an integral part of the day for many. Favourite dishes such as fried fish were frequently served along with items such as steak, lobster, cold meat salads and chicken. Breakfast, lunch and dinner were normally served and traditional high tea was a great favourite in many cruising areas.

**ABOVE** Passengers queuing on Ilfracombe Pier in Devon around 1907. Many passengers at the time would travel to and from their holiday destination complete with luggage. Piers such as the one at Ilfracombe were major paddle steamer hubs and it was always fascinating to watch the arrivals and departures of steamers during summer months. *Ron Jones Collection*

Pleasure steamers normally called at several places during their visit to the coast to enable more passengers to be picked up and to maximise revenue. This provided an exciting spectacle as ropes were thrown by deckhands and gangways were placed between steamer and pier. This was always enjoyed by passengers, most of whom eagerly crowded the rails to watch. A cruise would usually last for three or more hours before the final seaside destination was reached and the passengers were then given a few hours, or more, to enjoy the destination before rejoining the steamer for the journey home.

When a steamer called at its main seaside destination, it was usual for more holidaymakers to be boarded for a trip 'round the bay' for a couple of hours before the steamer arrived back at the pier to pick up its original passengers.

When the last passenger had disembarked at the end of the day, the ship had to be cleaned and got ready for the next day. Stores had to be loaded and within a few short hours the next group of passengers were ready to be loaded. There was rarely time to take things easy. Pleasure steamers usually operated six days a week during a season that usually lasted from Easter until October.

*'In 1907 my brother and I went to Yarmouth for the Whitsun weekend, travelling with the* Walton Belle *which was going to open the season. On her deck she carried the wooden hut which was erected annually on the quay at Yarmouth capped by a sign which read "Walton Belle Steamer Berth". It was duly bought back at the end of each season.'* (T. More, PSPS Collection)

*'New Palace Steamers were very lavish with their free travel passes and issued far more complimentary tickets than other operators. I was told that the reason to get more people on board was so that they would spend good money on catering and in the bars. It was also good publicity for a steamer to arrive at, say, Margate very well loaded – but not overcrowded. The* Royal Sovereign *carried 1,558 and she looked very poorly patronised if she carried 700 or fewer. There was definitely something in this free pass policy and I wondered why other companies weren't alive to it.'* (Tom Mace, PSPS Collection)

Most passengers usually spent only a day at the seaside each year as this was all they could afford but some operators offered weekend returns. These were often linked to longer trips, for instance to France where passengers could enjoy a few hours ashore. Coach tours or an extra coastal cruise were often organised as optional extras.

*'To while away the slow progress up river there were often sing-songs or impromptu concerts and much talent was revealed. Most of the contemporary song hits were varied and I came to know the words of many unorthodox versions. We sometimes carried cycling clubs, the members of which would cycle to the destination and come back by steamer. They often organised really good talent.'* (J. Paine, PSPS Collection)

Many passengers used pleasure steamers as a ferry service. This was particularly important in areas that were geographically remote or where transport links were poor, such as Cardiff and Penarth to Weston, and Wemyss Bay to Rothesay. Often, the pleasure steamer was the cheapest and fastest way to reach a holiday destination and it was quite common for passengers on these ferry services to carry several items of luggage for their holiday. Publicity material from the time often lists the maximum amount of baggage that could be carried.

Life aboard a paddle steamer was eventful and ever-changing as the steamer moved swiftly from pier to pier. Paddle steamers became a seasonal feature of life for many during their heyday.

**BELOW** atmospheric view aboard the *Bristol Queen* during the mid-1960s. A paddle steamer gave its passengers a heady mix of fresh air and the hiss of the foamy wash of the paddle wheels, as can be seen in this view. *PSPS Collection*

# 5

# Paddle Steamers at War

## World War 1

The ascendancy of the paddle steamer was dealt a massive blow when World War 1 was declared over the busy August bank holiday weekend in 1914. Services were immediately suspended.

'On my last trip aboard the Royal Sovereign *before the 1914 war I experienced a strange feeling of uncertainty as we met several warships anchored off Margate. I did not like those ships. As we left Margate, their crews stood to attention and* played 'God Save the King'. We dipped the flag and responded. I can picture Captain Shaw on the bridge with a sort of far-away look. Maybe he felt as I did. I was not to know that I would tread the decks of warships before walking those pleasant decks again.' (Edward Smith, PSPS Collection)

Paddle steamer fleets were soon requisitioned and around 70 steamers were pressed into service as minesweepers to patrol the ports and coast of the UK and places further away such as the Mediterranean. They were well suited to this role as their shallow draught allowed them to patrol shallow waters. However, this could be dangerous work and soon steamers were lost. *Brighton Queen* was one of the first to be sunk off the Belgium coast in 1915. This event was followed soon after by the loss of the *Lady Ismay* and *Duchess of Hamilton*. Further losses in the Mediterranean included steamers of the Red Funnel fleet, most notably the *Princess Mary* and *Duchess of York*.

The larger paddle steamers were also employed as troop ships to ferry significant numbers of troops to France and Belgium. The Thames-based *Golden Eagle* performed particularly well in this role.

The distinctive Belle Steamer fleet of the Thames and East Coast typified the service given by paddle steamers during the war. Each Belle Steamer spent around six weeks being fitted as a minesweeper. This included clearing all saloons and cabins and removing equipment required for the peacetime passenger trade. Windows and ports holes were also plated over and a navigating bridge was fitted,

**ABOVE** World War 1 broke out over the bank holiday when paddle steamer services were at their busiest and services were immediately suspended. Banners were placed over posters by P. & A. Campbell to inform passengers about changes to South Coast services due to the declaration of war. The company's *Glen Rosa* is seen at Ilfracombe during World War 1. *PSPS Collection*

**RIGHT** The Belle Steamer fleet saw significant action during World War 1. The company was keen to promote the heroic role of its steamers after the war ended and published this booklet to outline their proud wartime work. *PSPS Collection*

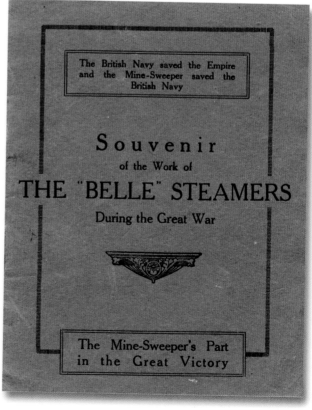

The British Navy saved the Empire and the Mine-Sweeper saved the British Navy

Souvenir
of the Work of

THE "BELLE" STEAMERS

During the Great War

The Mine-Sweeper's Part
in the Great Victory

**ABOVE** Paddle steamers from most UK fleets were quickly requisitioned when World War 1 broke out and again in 1939. Here, the *Southwold Belle* is seen during wartime service. Steamers were mainly used as minesweepers and troop carriers. *PSPS Collection*

**BELOW** The *Duke of Devonshire* (later to become the *Consul*) photographed during World War 1 alongside a coaling barge. This paddle steamer served as a minesweeper during the war. *PSPS Collection*

along with wireless facilities. Additional bunkers were also provided to carry up to 80 tons of coal. Hotchkiss submarine guns, searchlights and sweeper gear completed the refit.

Each minesweeper had around 40 crew. Some engineers were called up, whilst the peacetime captains were employed elsewhere as pilots to navigate channels.

The paddle steamers were then formed into small flotillas of about six steamers and each ship stayed at sea working for around a week at a time. The North Sea was particularly well-laden with enemy mines by the enemy. The paddle minesweepers at first encountered problems with the scale of operations, but as more and more steamers were converted for minesweeping the job became easier as they were able to destroy the mines as quick as they were laid.

*'Their work is gigantic. It is easy to talk of a mine-sweeper. I wish that the whole nation could understand what these ships are doing. The thousands of men engaged in the operations are men who are feeding the whole population of this country from morning till night, battling with the elements as well as with the enemy, fighting dangers overhead and dangers under the sea.'* (Sir Edward Carson, 1917, Belle Steamer Guide)

Nonetheless, there were casualties and the Bristol Channel fleet of P. & A. Campbell lost the *Brighton Queen* and *Lady Ismay* during action in 1915 and at the end of hostilities both the *Glen Rosa* and *Waverley* departed for the scrap yard as they were no longer fit for service. On the South Coast, the massive prewar fleet of 24 steamers suffered less

than other areas, but perhaps the saddest loss was the famed *Majestic* of the Cosens fleet.

The end of World War 1 in 1918 did not mean that paddle minesweepers were quickly dispersed. Work continued until early 1919 as the seas around the UK had to be made safe as such a large number of mines had been laid.

*'It is impossible to realise the magnificent and efficient work which was being done by the small craft engaged in sweeping the seas of mines sown broadcast by the enemy.'* (Earl of Lytton, House of Lords, 1917, Belle Steamer Guide)

## World War 2

Inevitably, the outbreak of World War 2 in September 1939 saw most pleasure steamers once again take up a wartime role. Many were mobilised just before the declaration of war to help with the evacuation of over 20,000 children. As most paddle steamers were located close to the potential targets of major cities and ports, they performed a crucial role in taking children to safety elsewhere. Vessels such as

**BELOW** Just a few months after her maiden voyage in May 1939 (shown here), *Royal Daffodil* was requisitioned to transport evacuee children from London and Thames-side towns to the safety of East Coast resorts such as Lowestoft. Around 2,000 children were aboard for each trip and they were entertained with deck games such as quoits. Others went to view the engine room. Despite being a dangerous trip, many found the experience a great adventure.
*Andrew Gladwell Collection*

**ABOVE** The *Lorna Doone* after her refit as a minesweeper at H.M. Dockyard Devonport in 1940. She later took up duties with the Harwich Flotilla sweeping for mines in the Thames Estuary and staving off the odd German attack. 'Lord Haw Haw' claimed a couple of times that the *Lorna Doone* had been sunk. *PSPS Collection*

**BELOW** *Medway Queen* during World War 2. You can clearly appreciate the minesweeping gear in this view. Her fame was gained through the heroism of her crew during the miracle of Dunkirk when she rescued over 7,000 troops. Four gallantry awards were awarded to her at Dunkirk. She made seven crossings to the beaches during the evacuation. *PSPS Collection*

**ABOVE** *Medway Queen* in wartime camouflage at Dover around 1940. *Medway Queen*, like so many other pleasure steamers, provided a vital role during wartime. Her steady peacetime career was a stark contrast to the action that she faced in wartime. Her title of 'Heroine of Dunkirk' did a great deal to save her for preservation when her Medway service came to an end. *PSPS Collection*

the *Royal Daffodil*, *Golden Eagle* and *Queen of the Channel* all played their part. This was to be the first war where the home front was directly threatened by the enemy. The evacuation of children from places such as Gravesend and Woolwich was an emotional experience but humour was also present, especially when a famed Thames skipper ended up at his final destination with more passengers than he had set out with. The simple reason for this was that women had given birth on the steamer en route!

Once the evacuation had taken place, the numerous paddle and pleasure steamers were acquired by the Royal Navy for wartime service. There were two main uses for the steamers: the larger craft would be used as troop carriers whilst the smaller vessels made better minesweepers, being admirably suited to this role as they had excellent manoeuvrability in shallow water. Refits quickly took place and by early 1940 over 30 paddle steamers had been refitted

as minesweepers. A paddle minesweeper towed a search rig at the stern. This in turn cut wires mooring the mines to release the mines to the surface. The minesweeper then fired upon the mines to detonate them. In addition, these vessels had a range of guns fitted to protect them should they encounter the enemy.

Paddle minesweepers were placed at five major ports in the UK. Dover had the largest concentration of them. Often, their peacetime master and officers were called-up to operate them and an amazing total of over 50 pleasure steamers were called requisitioned during the war.

Very quickly, the steamers encountered their greatest drama when they faced the challenge of Dunkirk in May 1940. The evacuation of the forces from the beaches of Dunkirk was an unexpected opportunity for the pleasure steamer to show its versatility, and the crews performed with heroism. The shallow draft of the paddle steamers which enabled them to work close to the shore made them perfect candidates for evacuating large numbers of troops quickly. Well-loved steamers such as the *Crested Eagle*, *Brighton Belle*, *Royal Daffodil*, *Waverley*, *Golden Eagle* and *Queen of the Channel* joined the myriad of small boats to rescue troops from the beaches whilst under intense fire. For many, the onslaught of enemy bombing was too

**ABOVE** The 1899-built *Waverley* was sunk at Dunkirk. She was part of the 12th Minesweeping Flotilla that was based at Harwich and lost when going to the assistance of the *Eagle III*. The present *Waverley* was built as a replacement in 1946 with compensation awarded by the government for the loss of the 1899 vessel.

*John Gilmore Collection*

**BELOW** *Royal Daffodil* undergoing repairs to wartime damage. The '*Daffodil*' suffered almost catastrophic damage at Dunkirk but miraculously survived. She rescued 9,500 men during the Dunkirk evacuation but on 2 June 1940 a bomb passed straight through her. A temporary patch of mattresses and wood was applied and this saved the ship. In addition to the bomb, *Royal Daffodil* survived machine-gun and torpedo attack. She later took up regular troop-carrying duties at Stranraer and performed admirably in that role.

*Andrew Gladwell Collection*

ABOVE Another view of the *Medway Queen*. When she was later withdrawn and her future seemed unsure, many of the troops she had rescued at Dunkirk went to her aid and promoted her preservation. *PSPS Collection*

RIGHT Pleasure steamer enthusiasts inspect one of the wrecked lifeboats from *Royal Sovereign*, which sank in the Bristol Channel after hitting a mine. *Royal Sovereign* had earlier helped to evacuate large numbers of children at the start of the war. She had also taken part at Dunkirk. *PSPS Collection*

much. The *Crested Eagle* was hit and sunk dramatically. Her fuel oil ignited, resulting in the death of over 300, including troops and crew. The almost new *Queen of the Channel* was also bombed and sunk. The 1899 *Waverley* was another loss but rescued her first group of troops before returning to Dunkirk. She came under heavy aircraft attack and was badly damaged, sinking with the loss of around 350 lives. On that day, Captain John Cameron DSC was aboard her, who was later to become the first master of the replacement *Waverley* in 1947. *Royal Daffodil* was hit by a bomb on her final trip to pick up troops and suffered significant damage to one of her engines. She limped home and hasty repairs managed to save her. The almost new *Gracie Fields* was another loss. With significant damage to her engine room and no

rudder, attempts to tow her home failed and she sank.

The significant role that the pleasure steamers played at the beaches of Dunkirk cannot be underestimated. One of the larger steamers, the *Royal Daffodil*, saved 9,500 troops and the small *Medway Queen* became known as the 'Heroine of Dunkirk' as she managed to rescue over 7,000 troops on seven trips to the beaches, which was a remarkable feat considering her relatively small size.

When the BBC announced the successful evacuation of Dunkirk on 5 June 1940 it seemed a somewhat subdued 'victory'. The miracle of Dunkirk was the seaside pleasure

**FACING PAGE TOP** P. & A. Campbell's *Britannia* returns to Bristol in May 1945 after wartime service. Renamed as HMS *Skiddaw*, she was stationed on the Tyne and assisted in the Normandy landings by guarding sections of the Mulberry Harbour at Dungeness Bay. She also protected convoys with anti-aircraft cover along the East Coast to the River Thames and the English Channel. *PSPS Collection*

**FACING PAGE BOTTOM** Crew rescued by P. & A. Campbell's *Glen Gower* off the East Coast in October 1940. Paddle steamers performed a valuable service during both world wars but, sadly, many famous steamers were lost during the conflicts. Whilst many saw action, others provided much needed ferry and accommodation services. *PSPS Collection*

**ABOVE RIGHT** *Ryde* was requisitioned in 1939 for conversion to a paddle minesweeper. She was later converted to a coastal auxiliary ack-ack vessel in 1942, when her sweeping gear was removed. The government allowed her to return to her peacetime role in July 1945. *Andrew Gladwell*

**RIGHT** Brass plaque from the *Bournemouth Queen*. It was made to commemorate the war service of the steamer during World War 2 and acknowledges the work undertaken by Thornycroft in re-conditioning the vessel afterwards. The plaque was in place on board the steamer for many years until she was withdrawn, and is now part of the PSPS collection. *PSPS Collection*

steamer's finest hour but so many fondly loved and magnificent pleasure steamers had been lost. Nevertheless, the 25 large pleasure steamers at Dunkirk had rescued a total of 309,739 men, superbly demonstrating the vessels' resilience, versatility and capability. The heroism of their crews was not forgotten and even today the remaining steamers such as the *Medway Queen* and *Princess Elizabeth* are still remembered for their deeds in such a dark hour in Britain's history.

The surviving steamers were quickly repaired after Dunkirk and resumed their planned wartime roles. Larger steamers such as the *Royal Daffodil* quietly carried out their role transporting troops although some vessels were still lost later in the war. *Royal Sovereign* was sunk by a mine in the Bristol Channel and the *City of Rochester* was bombed in the Medway but these were relatively isolated incidents compared to Dunkirk.

The number of paddle steamers involved in minesweeping duties was reduced during the latter part of the war and their duties became less dangerous. The *Bournemouth Queen*, *Duchess of Rothesay* and *Eagle III* became accommodation ships. Others became anti-aircraft vessels and helped to fight off enemy aircraft at various places around the coast of the UK.

Some steamers performed wartime duties of an altogether different type as they continued ferry services at key areas around the UK. The Firth of Clyde always had a great need for paddle steamers to ferry people to the various remote calling points of the Firth. The vintage *Lucy Ashton* performed heroically during those wartime years as she quietly ferried well over one million people on the Firth of Clyde. Close-by, on Loch Lomond, the steamers *Prince Edward* and *Princess May* performed a vital duty as land-locked steamers when they provided accommodation for families bombed by the Luftwaffe. At the other end of the country, the distinctive River Dart paddle steamers undertook ferry duties for the US Navy as well as providing normal ferry services at other times.

As peace grew closer, it became apparent that the pleasure steamer fleet was greatly depleted from that of 1939. The steamers that had survived had undergone six years of extremely hard work and were in a poor condition. For many, this was the first time that they had not just operated in fine, sunny summer months but instead had been working all-year round, often in bad weather and under fierce enemy fire. It would take a great deal of commitment and money to re-equip the wartime fleet for the demobbed soldiers and their families who would soon want a carefree day at Rothesay or Southend.

6

# Postwar Decline

**ABOVE** *Jeanie Deans* at Craigendoran on 30 June 1964. The Firth of Clyde was
a wonderful example of where paddle steamer services linked with adjacent train
services. Both were able to thrive through excellent interlinking timetables that
enabled passengers to travel easily around a remote location. Paddle steamer
services survived on the Firth of Clyde longer than other in areas of the UK.

*PSPS Collection*

When World War 2 ended, operators eagerly grasped government compensation for their wartime losses and promptly set about renovating their fleets or building new pleasure steamers that were more or less identical to those that had been lost. At the time, this seemed to be a sensible move as people wanted to resume their peacetime lives. It was assumed that things would be just as they were in the late 1930s. Demobbed servicemen quickly returned to 'Civvy Street' and seaside resorts around the coast of the UK experienced a massive boom in popularity during the late 1940s. Many new pleasure steamers entered service at this time, and vessels such as *Bristol Queen*, *Royal Sovereign*, *Queen of the Channel* and *Cardiff Queen* soon became well loved. Yet these large new steamers were to become uneconomic within a decade.

By the start of the 1950s, operators had brought all of the new pleasure steamers into service but their revitalised fleets were no longer what was wanted as their passengers moved increasingly away to the motor car and air travel. World War 2 had seen advances in engineering and manufacture which meant that motoring was becoming more affordable. People had also seen more of the world and many aspects of their lives were changing rapidly compared to their parents' generation.

The 1950s and 1960s witnessed the rapid decline of the pleasure steamer in the UK which was almost terminal. For some, the steamers were relics of the past and their demise was 'sad and inevitable'. The loss was set against a world where many other forms of transport were flourishing. The family car, with its flexibility and non-reliance on weather, was attractive to an increasing number of families. The car had been eating away at the traditional steamer market for several decades, but now car ownership became available to more people than ever before. People's tastes were changing and they were becoming more affluent and not tied to tradition as their parents had been, epitomised by the coming of the teenager. New entertainment such as television showed a wider world than that of a generation earlier. Rationing of goods such as petrol also gave people the 'feel good' factor, allowing them to fully embrace the freedom of the motor car.

Media, advertising and increasing consumerism were making folk aware that they had a choice of where to spend their holiday. For the first time, many people were looking towards more distant holidays in the UK and for some the possibility of a foreign holiday was an achievable option.

As the 1950s progressed, almost every pleasure steamer fleet in the UK declined. Every month and year bought news of another old favourite steamer being withdrawn from service and eventually scrapped. Those that survived faced an ever more uncertain future.

## The Thames and Medway

When World War 2 finished, only six pleasure steamers were available for service on the River Thames, compared with thirteen at the outbreak of the conflict. However, the remaining steamers were quickly reconditioned and in 1946 the *Royal Eagle* inaugurated services again from London. The remainder of the old fleet returned a year later in 1947. The next year was significant for the Thames fleet as the new *Queen of the Channel* entered service, to be followed a year later by the new *Royal Sovereign*. Both were built by the renowned Denny of Dumbarton, joining the *Royal Daffodil* of 1939 which was another product of the Denny yard. A prominent feature of both new steamers was the side blisters that flared out on either side of the hull to increase passenger space.

*Golden Eagle* was withdrawn in 1950. It was rumoured that the *Golden Eagle* or *Royal Eagle* would see further service on the South Coast for P. & A. Campbell in 1951, but these came to nothing and *Royal Eagle* was not commissioned for the year. Instead, the two grand ladies of the General Steam Navigation Company fleet were scrapped, the splendid *Royal Eagle* being less than 20 years old.

The 1950s were a decade of dwindling trade on the Thames. Smaller vessels such as the *Crested Eagle* and *Medway Queen* maintained regular services whilst the three large motor ships, *Royal Daffodil*, *Royal Sovereign* and *Queen of the Channel* continued on various routes with regular calls to Boulogne and Calais after the bans on calling at these ports were lifted in the mid 1950s.

**ABOVE** Advertisement for Eagle Steamer services from London aboard the *Golden Eagle*, *Royal Eagle* and *Royal Sovereign* in 1949. By this time, the days of the paddle steamer were numbered on the Thames and, shortly after, they were withdrawn.
*Andrew Gladwell Collection*

**ABOVE AND RIGHT** Rare views showing the construction of the *Bristol Queen* at the Charles Hill yard at Bristol between 1945 and 1946. They show the ribs in place and hull plates gradually being positioned. Paddle steamers were built after the end of the war with government compensation for wartime losses. *PSPS Collection*

**FACING PAGE TOP** Cosens, unlike most other operators around the UK, had not suffered losses during World War 2. However, although its paddle steamers were a lot smaller than many others, the company was still affected by declining revenues after the war and its fleet shrank as a result. *PSPS Collection*

**FACING PAGE BOTTOM** *Royal Daffodil's* withdrawal heralded the end of the long tradition of Thames pleasure steamers operated by the General Steam Navigation Company as *Royal Sovereign* and *Queen of the Channel* followed soon after. *Andrew Gladwell Collection*

**RIGHT** Major royal occasions such as coronations have notably been marked by Spithead fleet reviews. In June 1953, most of the remaining UK pleasure steamer fleet assembled to mark the coronation of Queen Elizabeth II and this special menu from the *Cardiff Queen* was used on the steamer. *Balmoral* is now the last operating large pleasure steamer that was present at the 1953 review. *PSPS Collection*

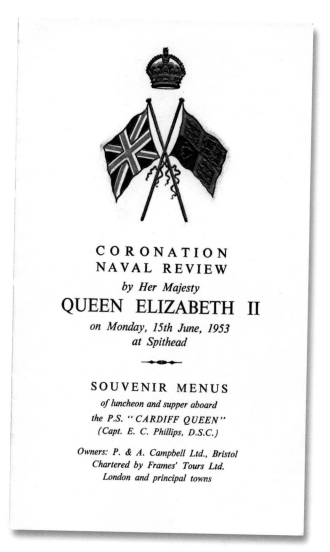

CORONATION
NAVAL REVIEW
*by Her Majesty*
QUEEN ELIZABETH II
*on Monday, 15th June, 1953
at Spithead*

SOUVENIR MENUS
*of luncheon and supper aboard
the P.S. " CARDIFF QUEEN"
(Capt. E. C. Phillips, D.S.C.)*

*Owners: P. & A. Campbell Ltd., Bristol
Chartered by Frames' Tours Ltd.
London and principal towns*

'Medway Queen *spent most of her career on the Medway and Thames but on occasions made journeys further afield, for instance at the 1953 Spithead review. I sailed on the* Royal Daffodil *from London to Southampton and reaching the Straits of Dover ran into fog . . . commiserations all round about poor* Medway Queen *which had left Chatham at the same time that we had left Deptford. We had radar etc and were able to avoid a considerable amount of the weather but nothing so modern on the* Medway Queen. *When we reached the Nab and went into Southampton Water, what should we see ahead of us by the* Medway Queen! *She had paddled right through the bad weather and was well ahead of us all!'* (John Richardson, 1963, PSPS Collection)

GSNC reacted to the drop in trade during the 1950s by introducing gimmicks such as rock and roll cruises, jazz jamborees and bingo. These could never halt the decline and the company, like the others around the UK coast, could merely watch the gradual cessation of services with a spirit of helpless acceptance. The gloom was, though, interspersed with items of good news such as the opening of Deal Pier to steamer services in 1957. This was balanced by the closure of Chatham Sun Pier and Sheerness Pier. Day trips to France saw a respectable rise during the late 1950s as the idea of a day cruise to France was still a novelty to many. Attractive publicity material helped this service thrive. The most popular and lucrative services remained those from London to the Kent and Essex resorts but the underlying problem was as much to do with the final destination as the traditional British seaside resort was losing its former glory and hotels and piers were starting to decline and close.

In the early 1960s the GSNC ambitiously introduced continental holidays by steamer and coach. These were offered to such far-flung places as Paris and Spain, with journeys taking around 24 hours in each direction. No wonder air travel would be so appealing to travellers a decade later! GSNC was now lumbered with a fleet that was too big for its needs in the form of the three large motor ships. They were superb, comfortable and very seaworthy vessels, but on a financial basis could not sustain the dwindling business that they faced. The smaller *Medway Queen* was withdrawn first and in September 1963 made her farewell calls at the Kent and Essex piers that she had served for four decades. In Christmas 1966 an announcement was made that GSNC services were to cease. The well-loved *Royal Daffodil* was the first to go to the scrap yard and the two other Thames pleasure steamers followed soon after.

## South Coast

After the upheaval of World War 2, the operators on the South Coast quickly attempted to start pleasure steamer services again. All of the pleasure pier embarkation points had been breached during the conflict to stop invasion, which meant that a great amount of rebuilding work had to

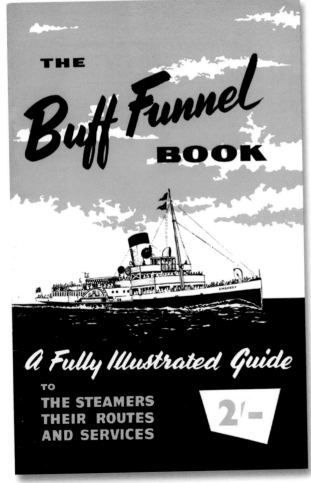

THE *Buff Funnel* BOOK

A Fully Illustrated Guide
TO
THE STEAMERS
THEIR ROUTES
AND SERVICES

2/-

**ABOVE** The well-loved *Embassy* at Bournemouth Pier. *Embassy* had been built in 1911 and had operated to the Isle of Wight before being acquired by Cosens in the inter-war years. She became the final Cosens paddle steamer to operate regularly from Bournemouth Pier. *PSPS Collection*

**LEFT** Small guides were sold aboard the Cosens paddle steamers to give passengers ideas about what to do when they got to their final destination They also acted as guides to places of interest along the way. *Andrew Gladwell*

be done before things could get back to normal. The pleasure steamers also needed to be refitted for peacetime trade rather than wartime service. In 1946 Cosens of Weymouth was acquired by Red Funnel of Southampton, but continued to operate its fleet independently until services ceased in the mid-1960s. Cosens had lost none of its fleet of steamers during the war and placed *Victoria* and *Empress* back in service in 1946 at Weymouth. *Princess Elizabeth* followed shortly after for Red Funnel and by 1947 *Monarch* and *Embassy* were also back operating between the familiar Cosens destinations. Eventually, in 1948, *Consul* and *Emperor of India* re-entered service, both boasting an enclosed wheelhouse for the first time. Sensibly, Cosens did not expand its fleet during those post-war years when the future was uncertain.

ABOVE *Consul* arriving at Weymouth with the spectacular Dorset coastline in the background. *Consul* was a charming and historic little steamer. After withdrawal, she faced an uncertain future before being scrapped. *PSPS Collection*

BELOW *Embassy* during her final years as a member of the Cosens of Weymouth fleet. Day trips to the Isle of Wight were very popular. She became the final paddle steamer in the Cosens fleet. *PSPS Collection*

Red Funnel was in a different position as several of its steamers had been lost or were unsuitable for further service. Small second-hand steamers were acquired to provide Solent cruises but they were just a stop-gap. Large steamers to replace wartime losses were soon placed in service, with the *Lorna Doone* working out of Bournemouth and *Solent Queen* providing additional excursion services.

In 1949 the South Coast services were enlivened when Red Funnel placed the order for one of its most well-loved and long-lived vessels. The

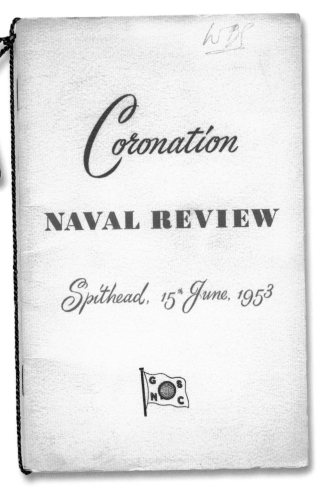

**RIGHT** Royal events created great excitement amongst passengers especially in the days before television. Fleet Reviews at Spithead were quite spectacular and included fleets moored in lines for inspection and illuminations and fireworks at night. This souvenir programme is from the Coronation Fleet Review in 1953 and was issued by the General Steam Navigation Company. *Andrew Gladwell Collection*

**FACING PAGE** The splendid *Consul* at Weymouth Pleasure Pier. This small Victorian paddle steamer was significantly different from the vast modern motor vessels that were operating at such places as the River Thames at the time. *PSPS Collection*

**ABOVE** *Balmoral* was built for Red Funnel in 1949 and provided a ferry service between Southampton and Cowes on the Isle of Wight. She also provided pleasure cruises during the summer months. *PSPS Collection*

**FACING PAGE TOP** *Swanage Queen* alongside Bournemouth Pier. She ran cruises to Swanage and to the Isle of Wight from the pier in 1961. *PSPS Collection*

**FACING PAGE BOTTOM** *Embassy* during her postwar heyday. *Monarch, Consul* and *Embassy* were the three famous paddle steamers operated by Cosens in postwar years. *Andrew Gladwell Collection*

**RIGHT** *Princess Elizabeth* was built for service for Red Funnel in 1927. After withdrawal by the company she faced an uncertain future but is now preserved at Dunkirk. She has now spent more years in preservation than operation. *PSPS Collection*

**BELOW** P. & A. Campbell operated paddle steamers along the Sussex coast until the mid 1950s. 'No Passport' day trips to France were always popular. *PSPS Collection*

motor ship *Balmoral*, ordered from the Thornycroft yard, was built to provide the ferry service between Southampton and Cowes but her exceptional design, facilities and seaworthiness were also suited to the extensive excursion and cruise work that she carried out during the summer months.

By the 1950s, pleasure steamers on the South Coast were starting to be sold or withdrawn. *Lorna Doone* was one of the first to disappear in 1951 and *Victoria* of the Cosens fleet followed shortly after. The postwar fleets were now leaner to reflect the new conditions facing the business but there were some new vessels, most notably the Portsmouth railway fleet of *Southsea, Shanklin* and *Brading*. These were well-built vessels with an excellent mix of open and enclosed passenger accommodation. The year 1951 also saw the arrival of the *Monarch*. Originally built as the *Shanklin* for the Southern Railway, she became a well-loved member of the Cosens fleet in the 1950s.

By the mid-1950s the postwar shrinkage of fleets was becoming acute. P. & A. Campbell became an early casualty of the decline and by 1956 had withdrawn its services on the Sussex Coast. The following year, *Emperor of India* was

**ABOVE** *Balmoral* was built for Red Funnel to operate the Southampton to Isle of Wight service in 1949 at a cost of £154,750. She had a dual role as a ferry and summer excursion ship. Her deck at the stern was open so that she could accommodate up to 12 cars on a crossing. One of her most memorable cruises for Red Funnel was to witness the departure of the liner *Queen Mary* from Southampton for the final time in 1967. *PSPS Collection*

**RIGHT** Cover for Red Funnel's souvenir brochure from the 1950s. The cover shows the *Balmoral*. The company house flag shows in its quarters four of the original fleet members of 1861 – *Pearl*, *Ruby*, *Sapphire* and *Emerald*. *PSPS Collection*

**FACING PAGE** *Consul* in Weymouth harbour in 1964. She returned to Weymouth in competition with the *Princess Elizabeth*. Sadly, paddle steamer business had shrunk considerably by that time which meant that two steamers could not survive. *PSPS Collection*

**ABOVE** *Consul* at Lulworth Cove. The Cosens fleet of paddle steamers provided popular steamer cruises along the scenic Dorset coastline for a hundred years. The picturesque Lulworth Cove was a wonderful destination for paddle steamers and passengers were landed along a ramp onto the beach. *Consul* experienced a great deal of uncertainty after being withdrawn by Cosens after the 1962 season, and despite valiant attempts to preserve her she was scrapped in 1968.

*PSPS Collection*

withdrawn by Cosens and *Bournemouth Queen* followed shortly after. By the end of the 1950s the Red Funnel excursion fleet had shrunk dramatically, with just *Balmoral*, *Princess Elizabeth* and *Vecta* carrying on the cruising tradition.

By now, the Cosens and Red Funnel excursion fleets were a pale reflection of their former selves. Luckily, Red Funnel had started to change from carrying passengers to cars, giving it options for the future with the introduction of car ferries. *Princess Elizabeth* – the last of the Red Funnel paddle steamers – was sold from the fleet to operate from

Torquay and Dorset in 1959 and by 1965 *Balmoral* was the last Red Funnel excursion steamer.

After *Empress* was taken out of service in 1955, Cosens had only three paddle steamers running in its final years: *Consul*, *Embassy* and *Monarch*. *Embassy* and *Monarch* mainly operated out of Bournemouth whilst *Consul* was principally linked to Weymouth. With postwar refits, all three steamers happily plied for Dorset coast trade throughout the 1950s. *Monarch* was the first to depart for the breakers yard in 1961. Herbert Jennings' *Swanage Queen* (ex-*Freshwater*), which had been operated along the Sussex Coast, attempted to pick up some of the business in Dorset. But the market was weak, the venture with *Swanage Queen* failed and she was taken out of service at the end of the 1962 season. *Princess Elizabeth* had a final fling with cruises out of Bournemouth and Weymouth in 1962 but *Consul* was offered for sale in the same year and after a short career operating along the Sussex Coast she returned to Weymouth in 1964 before being sold as an accommodation vessel.

**ABOVE** *Embassy* departing from Yarmouth on 28 June 1963. In 1966, *Embassy* suffered mechanical and other problems and operated her final cruise for Cosens on 22 September of that year. After withdrawal, she was sold for scrap and departed Weymouth under tow on 25 May 1967 for scrapping in Belgium, where she arrived on 28 May 1967.
*John Gilmore*

**LEFT** *Embassy*, along with *Consul* and *Monarch*, formed the famous post-war trio of steamers of the Cosens of Weymouth fleet. They provided a fine service that linked the seaside resorts of Dorset to the Solent and the Isle of Wight. They were steamers with great character. *Embassy* became the last Cosens paddle steamer and was withdrawn in 1966. *PSPS Collection*

The early 1960s saw a great shrinking of the Red Funnel and Cosens fleets on the South Coast and the Portsmouth paddle steamers were, of course, facing similar problems. This view was taken aboard the *Ryde* in May 1964. *Ryde* was withdrawn in 1969 and purchased by two Isle of Wight businessmen. In September 1970 she started a new career as a nightclub and was renamed as *Ryde Queen*. She replaced the *Medway Queen* at Binfield Marina on the River Medina, close to Newport. *John Gilmore*

**LEFT** 'No Passport' trips to France from places such as Brighton were always popular. P. & A. Campbell and the General Steam Navigation Company were the principal operators of these services and often also offered coach trips from Boulogne and Calais to take passengers on short tours of places such as the military cemeteries and battlefields. *PSPS Collection*

**FACING PAGE TOP** *Waverley* was built at the A. & J. Inglis yard and was launched on 2 October 1946 by Lady Matthews who was the wife of Sir Ronald Matthews, Chairman of the LNER. *Waverley* cost £160,000 to build and her first master was Captain John Cameron DSC. She entered Firth of Clyde service on Monday 16 June 1947. The cost of her 'Three Lochs' tour was 15 shillings first class and 12 shillings second class. *Andrew Gladwell Collection*

**FACING PAGE BOTTOM** *Waverley's* interior in the late 1940s was austere but stylish and the steamer was originally a two-class steamer. During her early preservation career her interiors were modernised. These were later restored to their 1940s design during her 'Heritage Rebuild' in 2000. *Andrew Gladwell Collection*

**BELOW LEFT** During the 1960s, the drink manufacturer Lawson's produced a series of attractive labels for its bottles of soft drinks. Many of the Firth of Clyde fleet such as *Jeanie Deans*, *Waverley* and *Maid of the Loch* were depicted on labels to represent different flavours. *Andrew Gladwell Collection*

*Princess Elizabeth* failed soon after and her days as an operating paddle steamer ended. Sadly, by 1966, *Embassy*, the last of the three postwar favourites, ended her Cosens career and was scrapped.

## Firth of Clyde

The Firth of Clyde fleet, like all others in the UK, suffered during World War 2 and several well-loved pleasure steamers were lost. One of these was the *Waverley*, lost at Dunkirk. An order was soon placed for a replacement *Waverley*, built by the Inglis yard for LNER services on the Firth of Clyde. She became the last paddle steamer to be built for Firth of Clyde service and was launched in October 1946. She entered service in June 1947 and cruised on the route for which she had been built – up Loch Goil and Loch Long to Arrochar and Lochgoilhead.

When the railways were nationalised in 1948, all LNER and LMS pleasure steamers were operated for the first time by the British Transport Commission. This resulted in a change of livery and the bright red, black and white funnels of steamers such as *Waverley* were soon replaced with a more austere buff and black.

By the start of the 1950s, the British Transport Commission wanted to modernise the Clyde fleet as it was

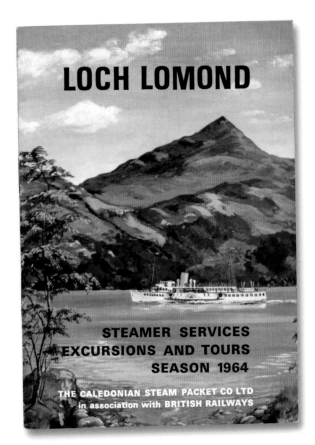

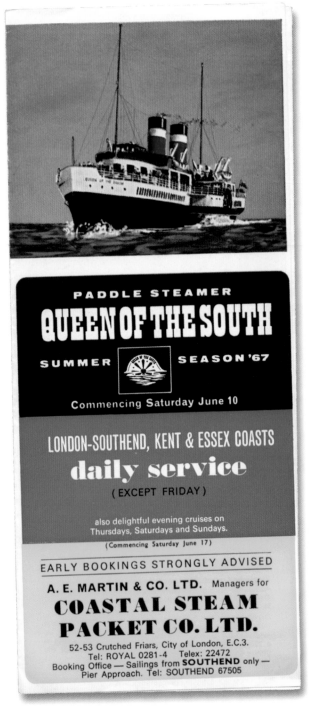

ABOVE On the Firth of Clyde and Loch Lomond paddle steamers
were lucky in that they normally provided the fastest services
to locations because of their inaccessibility. They were therefore
able to keep going for longer than other areas around the UK.
*Maid of the Loch* provided a service from Balloch to Ardlui at the
northern end of the loch. Later, her final call was a few miles short
of this at Inversnaid, from where she would then cruise to the head
of the loch. *Andrew Gladwell Collection*

clear that the fleet in the future would have more of a role as
ferries carrying cars rather than the traditional daytripper
trade. Inevitably, several small and remote piers were
earmarked for closure and the piers at Strone and Kilmun
were soon shut. By 1952 older steamers started to be
withdrawn and within a year, the four 'Maids' motor vessels
entered service; they were named *Maid of Argyll, Maid of
Skelmorlie, Maid of Ashton* and *Maid of Cumbria*. They were
followed shortly after by the new general purpose vessels that
could carry a sizeable number of cars. The *Maid of the Loch*
was the final large traditional paddle steamer to be built in
the UK. She was taken in sections from the Inglis yard by rail
and rebuilt at Balloch, entering Loch Lomond service in
1953. With a service speed of twelve knots, *Maid of the Loch*
provided a first class steamer service for her passengers.

The last bastion of large paddle steamer fleets, the Firth
of Clyde, had witnessed some modernisation before the
mid-1950s. The Firth was different to the rest of the UK in
that the geography of Western Scotland meant that the

ABOVE The venture to keep alive paddle steamer cruising on
the River Thames with *Queen of the South* (ex *Jeanie Deans*) was
admirable but, beset by a number of mechanical and other issues,
the attempt ended in failure in the year that this brochure was
produced. She left the Thames in December 1967 to be broken
up at Antwerp. *Andrew Gladwell Collection*

RIGHT The burnt out remains of the Firth of Clyde favourite
*Caledonia* next to Waterloo Bridge in London, shortly after the fire
that wrecked her in 1980. The fate for many old paddle steamers
after withdrawal was to become a floating bar, restaurant or night
club. Sadly, fire destroyed several and others became uneconomic
and were closed and later scrapped. *PSPS Collection*

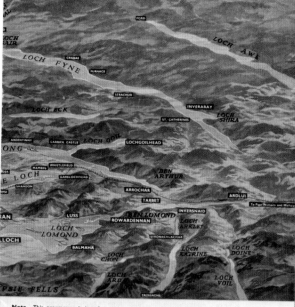

ADVANCE PROGRAMME OF

**PLEASURE SAILINGS
EXCURSIONS and TOURS**

in association with

BRITISH RAILWAYS

# FIRTH OF CLYDE
### AND
# LOCH LOMOND

Ist JUNE to 30th SEPTEMBER, 1963

Note.—This programme is issued to give intending passengers advance information regarding the principal point to point and excursion services which will operate during the period stated and may be subject to minor alteration. A booklet will be issued later giving more detailed information, including connecting train services and the full excursion programme.

**LEFT** The Caledonian Steam Packet Company usually showed a colour map on its brochures to show the many islands and lochs on the Firth of Clyde. The complex geography of the Firth meant that it was often confusing to know where you were as the steamer kept turning to reach its next destination. *PSPS Collection*

**BELOW** Label placed on bottles of lemon crush that were sold aboard the Clyde steamers on the Firth of Clyde around the 1960s. It shows the one of the favourite steamers of the Firth of Clyde – *Jeanie Deans*. After her withdrawal on the Clyde, she was sold in 1965 to enthusiasts on the River Thames and renamed as *Queen of the South*. Her original LNER livery was restored for her preservation career. *Andrew Gladwell Collection*

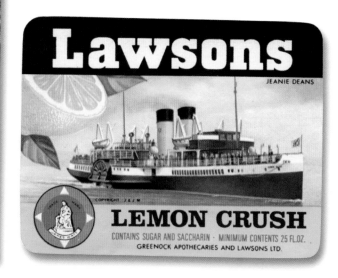

# Lawsons

JEANIE DEANS

## LEMON CRUSH

CONTAINS SUGAR AND SACCHARIN · MINIMUM CONTENTS 25 FL.OZ.
GREENOCK APOTHECARIES AND LAWSONS LTD.

*Waverley* at Craigendoran on 31 July 1967. Despite being just 20 years old at the time, *Waverley* was facing an uncertain future as the Firth of Clyde fleet contracted and increasing numbers of car ferries were being introduced. Craigendoran was the place that was always linked with *Waverley* during her initial years of service.
*Ron Jones*

*Maid of the Loch* continued operating on Loch Lomond throughout the 1970s but was ultimately withdrawn on 31 August 1981 as passenger numbers had dwindled and the service could no longer be sustained. The loch-side piers had also fallen into disrepair or had silted up. After several years of uncertainty, her future became positive in the 1990s when a charity gained ownership and restoration began. *Ron Jones*

to reflect several changes in ownership. All of a sudden, *Waverley* found herself alone as the last sea-going paddle steamer in the world.

Further changes in livery and name followed, but by the early 1970s the Firth of Clyde fleet had shrunk to just a few pleasure steamers and the tradition of Clyde cruising was more or less at an end. Although *Waverley* and *Queen Mary II* continued for a few years, services were curtailed in the 1970s. The *Maid of the Loch* continued on Loch Lomond but, with dwindling numbers of passengers, was finally withdrawn in 1981. Modern ferries then ruled the Firth of Clyde.

## Bristol Channel

The mid to late 1940s witnessed an 'Indian Summer' for the P. & A. Campbell fleet in the Bristol Channel as it took up the reigns again after the war with typical confidence. The company had suffered major losses during the conflict and the postwar fleet had been depleted by five paddle steamers but two splendid new paddle steamers were quickly ordered by P. & A. Campbell to help compensate for the casualties. They were the *Bristol Queen*, that had her trials in 1946, and the *Cardiff Queen* that followed shortly after in 1947. They were joined by the pleasure steamer *Empress Queen* that operated South Coast services in 1948. Originally seen as a cross-Channel vessel, she was never able to undertake this role as postwar restrictions meant she was unable to land passengers in France. Her time in this role was, therefore, brief before she was quickly withdrawn from service.

replacement of the steamer by car would never be totally viable there. The traditional Glasgow 'Doon the Watter' trade remained popular, in part due to the inaccessibility of island resorts. However, the 1960s saw many of the old favourites of the Firth of Clyde fleet withdrawn from service. Perhaps the most well loved of them all was the *Jeanie Deans*. She was sold in 1965 to London enthusiasts for further service on the Thames, although this venture later failed. *Talisman* was also scrapped in 1966. Meanwhile, *Caledonia* moved to Craigendoran to provide Bute services but by 1969, she was withdrawn and ended her days as a floating pub in London.

Whilst all of these changes were taking place, *Waverley's* timetable was regularly changed to reflect closure of piers and changes in passenger traffic. Her livery likewise changed

**TOP RIGHT** Menu for *Britannia's* farewell cruise to Ilfracombe. The sad event was marked by the publication of a poem to commemorate her departure. She was the flagship of the P. & A. Campbell fleet for most of her life. *Andrew Gladwell Collection*

**BOTTOM RIGHT** *Britannia's* farewell cruise to Ilfracombe on 19 September 1956 was a special event that included a superior buffet luncheon. She had served the company well for many years. *PSPS Collection*

**FACING PAGE TOP** The sponson area of the *Glen Gower* in May 1956. The P. & A. Campbell fleet was one of the most distinctive looking in the UK with its striking white and black livery. P. & A. Campbell reigned supreme over Bristol Channel services for almost a century and many of its paddle steamers lasted for most of the company's history. *PSPS Collection*

**FACING PAGE BOTTOM** *Balmoral* was acquired for further service with P. & A. Campbell after she ended her career with Red Funnel in the late 1960s. She became a popular pleasure steamer on the Bristol Channel and also ventured to North Wales to keep the 'White Funnel' tradition alive. She returned to the Bristol Channel in 1986 in a new livery to act as consort to the *Waverley*. *Andrew Gladwell*

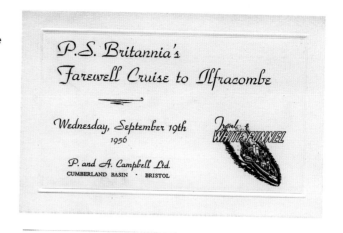

P. & A. Campbell ended the 1940s with the largest fleet of any pleasure steamer operator at the time, having seven large steamers at its disposal, and its confidence was such that it wanted to expand is fleet still further. Despite having this significant fleet, the company suffered the problems that beset the other operators around the UK in that most of the steamers were becoming old and required significant work to be done on them and the ever growing threat of the family motor car was affecting the potential for growth. The two new paddle steamers were, of course, splendid new ships, but their long-term future would be limited due to their size and uneconomic running.

Financial problems forced P. & A. Campbell to withdraw some of its fleet during the 1950s. In 1955 the *Ravenswood* was scrapped and was followed by the *Britannia* in 1956. By the end of the 1950s, P. & A. Campbell was in serious financial trouble and the company was taken over by George Nott Industries. Services did, however, continue into the 1960s but *Glen Gower* was later scrapped and *Glen Usk* became the last of the prewar paddle steamers to be withdrawn in 1960. In spite of this, the company ventured into North Wales cruising with the purchase of the *St Trillo* in 1962. She provided a good service for seven years in North Wales after the collapse of the Liverpool & North Wales Steamship Company at the end of the 1962 season.

At the end of the 1960s, P. & A. Campbell chartered other pleasure steamers, including the *Balmoral*, for further service on the traditional Campbell routes. The more economic motor ships spelled the death knell for the two large postwar paddle steamers. The majestic and almost new *Cardiff Queen* and *Bristol Queen* were scrapped just 20 years after they had entered service. Services by motor ships lingered on through the 1970s but the great days were by then over.

## North Wales

In North Wales, once the wartime grey paint had been removed from the three turbine steamers, *St Seiriol*, *St Tudno* and *St Trillo*, the Liverpool & North Wales Steamship Company recommended cruising very much to the timetable of prewar days. The first two steamers, however, quickly became too large for the postwar market. In 1961 *St Seiriol* was taken out of service and broken up, and in the following year the company was unable to continue and the long-established Liverpool & North Wales Steamship Co ceased trading. *St Tudno*, being a large and therefore an unattractive purchase for steamer operators, followed *St Seiriol* to the scrap yard. *St Trillo* was luckier and was acquired by P. & A. Campbell to keep cruising alive in North Wales. But enthusiasm and nostalgia were not enough to sustain profitability and, despite the support of motor ships in helping to keep tradition alive, services in North Wales had ceased by the late 1960s.

**ABOVE** *Cardiff Queen* departs from Ilfracombe while *Bristol Queen* is about to arrive during their final years of operation. Towns such as Ilfracombe welcomed the massive trade bought by the paddle steamers. *Bristol Queen* damaged a paddle wheel in August 1967 which led to her withdrawal and, despite a strong campaign to preserve her, she was broken up in 1968. *PSPS Collection*

**FACING PAGE TOP** Services were kept alive during the final years of North Wales and Bristol Channel operations by the *St Trillo*, *Balmoral* and *Westward Ho*. *Westward Ho* is shown here at Ilfracombe. She was similar in appearance to *Balmoral*. *Andrew Gladwell*

**FACING PAGE BOTTOM** Paddle steamers disappeared much earlier in North Wales than elsewhere. They were replaced with impressive turbine steamers such as the *St Seiriol*, *St Tudno* and *St Trillo* that proved to be more economic. By 1962, turbine steamer services had more or less ceased. *Andrew Gladwell Collection*

7

# Years of Restoration and Preservation

**ABOVE** *Glen Gower* at Cardiff in May 1956. Like the rest of the fleet, the *Glen Gower* faced
an uncertain future after the war and there were periods when she did not operate. She was
laid up after the 1957 season and three years later, in 1960, it was decided to dispose of her.
It seemed that the paddle steamer was facing extinction but luckily in 1959, the Paddle
Steamer Preservation Society was formed to try and halt the decline. *PSPS Collection*

At the end of the 1950s, the pleasure steamer was facing a terminal decline. However, many individuals and enthusiasts felt a strong degree of nostalgia about the paddle steamer and hoped that it could survive. The preservation movement was gaining popularity and in 1959 the Paddle Steamer Preservation Society (PSPS) was formed in an attempt to save the British paddle steamer, either through operation or by the preservation of material and memories connected with the vessels. The PSPS was originally inspired by the plan to withdraw the paddle steamer *Freshwater* at Lymington. Within months of its formation, the society found itself overwhelmed by the

**RIGHT** The Paddle Steamer Preservation Society was formed in 1959 to keep alive the paddle steamer in the UK. During its first decade, the society organised charter cruises such as this one on *Consul* in 1961 to halt the decline and to publicise services. *PSPS Collection*

**BELOW** The fate of the *Freshwater* led to the formation of the Paddle Steamer Preservation Society in 1959. She plied from Lymington to Yarmouth until being withdrawn. She then operated along the Sussex Coast as the *Sussex Queen*. After the failure of this venture, she was renamed yet again as *Swanage Queen* and operated from Bournemouth. This scheme also failed and soon after she was scrapped. *PSPS Collection*

ALL ABOARD!        DON'T MISS!

# ★ THE SPECIAL ★ EVENING CRUISE
### BY P.S. "CONSUL"
#### TOWARDS LULWORTH COVE

•  •  •

## FROM WEYMOUTH PIER
## WEDNESDAY, AUG., 16TH 1961

at   7.30 p.m.     (two hour cruise)

**Viewing Osmington, Ringstead and Durdle Dor, etc.**

•  •  •

**Competitions, Fun & Games For All**

## FARE 7/-   HALF PRICE CHILDREN
TICKETS AVAILABLE ON BOARD

### A 'PADDLE STEAMER PRESERVATION SOCIETY' CHARTER WHICH NO ONE SHOULD MISS

W. J. ADAMS (Bournemouth), LTD.

Medway Queen.

**RIGHT** A view aboard the *Medway Queen* towards the end of her career on the River Medway in Kent. This steamer changed very little over her 39-year career. She retained her open bridge until she was withdrawn in September 1963. Captain Leonard Horsham was her master when she ended her Medway career. *PSPS Collection*

**FACING PAGE TOP** *Medway Queen* departing from Southend just before her withdrawal in 1963. During those final days and weeks, *Medway Queen* generated a huge amount of emotion as she departed from the piers that she had known for so long. Bunting, cheers and speeches accompanied her during her final days and hours. *PSPS Collection*

**FACING PAGE BOTTOM** The 1950s were a decade of dwindling trade on the Thames. Nevertheless, smaller vessels such as the *Crested Eagle* and *Medway Queen* maintained regular services whilst the *Royal Daffodil*, *Royal Sovereign* and the *Queen of the Channel* continued on various routes with regular calls at Boulogne and Calais. These trips to France were boosted by the opening of Deal Pier in 1957 and by the lifting of restrictions on landing passengers in France in the mid-1950s. *Andrew Gladwell Ciollection*

scale of withdrawals and threats of closure. Enthusiasts were encouraged to lobby operators and the media and charter trips were also organised to try to revive interesting old routes and to give as much support as possible to struggling operators.

It was easy for preservationists to voice their concerns, but operators were plagued by old steamers needing expensive surveys and a significant amount of major work to give them a future that would last decades rather than months. Many paddle steamers had been built back in the Victorian era and by the 1950s had reached the end of their active life. They had simply had their time and, with the added wear and tear of wartime service, many were on their last legs. Their survival was possible, but it would need a lot of money and sheer guts to achieve any success at a time when the motor car and aircraft were trampling the opposition in their bid for supremacy.

The plight of paddle steamer preservation was focused during the early 1960s on the small estuary paddle steamer *Medway Queen*. The withdrawal of the Dunkirk veteran in September 1963 did a great deal to raise awareness that the paddle steamer was facing extinction.

'At Herne Bay many of the passengers went ashore and only a hundred or so enthusiasts and the pressmen remained onboard. Later there were 700 of us left aboard for the final sailing up the Medway but before we left, the Mayor of

*Southend paid a fitting tribute to the* Medway Queen *and the Southend Pier Concert Party sang "Now is the Hour" and other appropriate songs. Then with streamers flying all over the vessel and a great deal of noise, including rockets from the assembled hundreds, we slowly edged our way from the pier.'* (John Richardson, 1963, PSPS Collection)

With a damning diagnosis of 'old age and in need of attention', the months after withdrawal saw the *Medway Queen* face huge uncertainty over her future but very soon her exemplary wartime role was promoted and veteran groups as well as bodies such as the National Trust assisted the preservationists to try to secure her future. Time after time, options became exhausted as opposition was voiced or finances were unavailable. It was even proposed to moor *Medway Queen* alongside the piers at Blackpool or Great Yarmouth during the race to save her. It seemed that as soon as an option for her looked certain, then it all went wrong again.

**ABOVE** Paddle steamers like the *Ryde* have now spent around the same time out of service as they spent in service. From the 1980s onwards there was increasing optimism about the restoration of paddle steamers but many vessels had deteriorated for so long that the job of restoration had become much more serious and required vast amounts of money. *Andrew Gladwell*

**FACING PAGE TOP** *Medway Queen* at the East India Dock in London in June 1964. The months after her withdrawal witnessed a great frenzy of activity as enthusiasts attempted to keep her from the scrap yard. The preservation movement was in its infancy and had little experience of rescuing ships but its efforts ultimately saved the *Medway Queen*. *PSPS Collection*

**FACING PAGE BOTTOM** *Medway Queen* during her time on the Isle of Wight. After attempts to preserve *Medway Queen* in London failed, the ship faced being broken up. A last-minute reprieve was handed to her and she was towed to the Isle of Wight to operate as a floating club. *Medway Queen* showed that she was a survivor. *Andrew Gladwell*

The preservationists tried every avenue to ensure that the *Medway Queen* found a home away from the breakers yard. Stipulations in the sale document by the General Steam Navigation Company that stated that the steamer could not compete against its motor ship fleet meant that static preservation or scrapping were the most likely scenarios for her. One plan failed when Dolphin Square residents by the Thames in London opposed the licence for the *Medway Queen*, causing the Forte catering empire to withdraw its support. As the scrap yard torch moved ever closer, there was a last minute reprieve for the *Medway Queen* when she found a home as a club house for a marina on the River Medina on the Isle of Wight. At first, the Isle of Wight venture was a success as the *Medway Queen* sat alongside the later withdrawn Portsmouth paddle steamer *Ryde*. But, as debts rose, costs increased and her physical state deteriorated, the *Medway Queen* faced a period of significant uncertainty once again until the mid-1980s. This was worsened by a lack of clarity over ownership.

Some enthusiasts reacted to the withdrawal of paddle steamers with a great deal of enterprise. The 1960s still offered a glimmer of hope for the dwindling number of paddle steamers and attempts were made to operate them in areas other than where they had spent their main career. One such example was the *Consul* of the Cosens fleet. Once her Weymouth career had ended, *Consul* was operated by New Belle Steamers and provided a programme of cruises

NEW BELLE STEAMERS
ANNOUNCE A SERIES OF SPECIAL SEPTEMBER

## Sea Cruises from Southend

BY THE FAMOUS PADDLE STEAMER 'CONSUL'

Meals & Refreshments served in comfortable saloons at very reasonable prices. Music on Board

**FULLY LICENCED BAR OPEN ALL DAY**

| Tuesday 17th September | AT 12.15pm. Arr.Back App. 6.30 pm | **Day return to HERNE BAY** Allowing over 2 hours ashore. Passengers may also remain on board for special cruise from Herne Bay. | Day Return ONLY 9/6 Inc: Sea Cruise 14/- |
| | AT 6.30 pm. | **Single trip to GRAVESEND** Ample time to return by train & ferry to Southend. | Single Fare 4/6 |
| Wednesday 18th September | 3.45pm. Returning At App: 5.10pm. | **Delightful Afternoon Sea Cruise** To view the River Medway, Kentish Coast, Isles of Grain & Sheppey. | REDUCED Return Fare 4/- |
| | AT 5.15pm. Arriving Back About 9.00pm | **Musical SHOWBOAT Cruise** Special Evening Up River to **Gravesend and Tilbury** A wonderful opportunity to view the Illuminations. BAND ON BOARD    NON LANDING | Return Fare 8/6 |
| Thursday 19th September | AT 2.35pm Returning 4.15pm. | **Afternoon Sea Cruise** To view the Essex Coast, passing Shoeberryness Foulness & the Maplin Sands. | MIDWEEK Return Fare 4/- |
| | AT 4.15pm | **Single trip to Greenwich & London** Ample time to return by train to Southend. | Single Fare 6/- |
| Friday 20th September | AT 12.15pm Returning App: 6.30pm | **Day return to HERNE BAY** Allowing over 2 hours ashore. Passengers may also remain on board for special cruise from Herne Bay. | Day Return ONLY 9/6 Inc: Sea Cruise 14/- |
| | AT 6.30pm | **Single trip to GRAVESEND** Ample time to return by train & ferry to Southend. | Single Fare 4/6 |
| Saturday 21st September | 2.35pm Returning App: 3.40pm | **Afternoon Sea Cruise** Around the Estuaries of the Thames & Medway | Return Fare 4/- |
| | AT 3.45pm | **Single Trip to Greenwich & London** Ample time to return by train to Southend. | Single Fare 6/- |
| Final Sailings Sunday 22nd September | 2.35pm Returning App: 4.15pm | **Afternoon Sea Cruise** Up the Thames & over to the Medway to view Allhallows Canvey Island Shellhaven etc: | SPECIAL Return Fare 5/- |
| | AT 4.15pm | **Single trip to Greenwich & London** Ample time to return by train to Southend. | Single Fare 6/- |

All sailings subject to weather & circumstances permitting. Passengers are only carried on the terms & conditions printed on the back of the ticket.   Tickets available on the Steamer and in advance from:- 144 Sumner Rd. S.E.15   BER 3480   REDUCED FARE CHILDREN UNDER 14.

**ABOVE** The mid-1960s witnessed many valiant attempts to operate paddle steamers after they were withdrawn from service. Here, *Consul* is in the Pool of London during her short London season in September 1963. This was a failure, but it gave valuable experience for preservation attempts in the future. *PSPS Collection*

**LEFT** *Consul* provided a brief schedule of cruises from Southend during the 1963 season. By this time, she was an elderly steamer and her career was more or less at an end. She did, though, valiantly soldier on to provide a glimpse of what would be possible in the years ahead with a brief season of varied paddle steamer cruises. *Andrew Gladwell Collection*

**RIGHT** The small Neyland ferry *Alumchine* was seen by many to be the perfect candidate for preservation by the Paddle Steamer Preservation Society in the initial years after its formation. Sadly, though, negotiations came to nothing and the *Alumchine* was later scrapped. *PSPS Collection*

along the Sussex coast and on the River Thames during 1963. This admirable venture met with little success. It did, though, allow the enthusiasts to gain valuable experience to deal with future preservation attempts.

Another solution was to use the withdrawn pleasure steamers as static bars and restaurants and these flourished in 1960s and 1970s. Very soon, there were more steamers providing this role than there were operating.

By the middle of the 1960s, the preservation movement had grown significantly from its origins. Through the experience with the *Medway Queen* and other steamers, the PSPS realised that perhaps the best way to keep the tradition alive would be to keep a steamer in operation. This would of course be full of risk for an enthusiast group. But, a handful of talented people came together to look at preserving an example of the dying breed. It was a time when there were plenty of suitable candidates for preservation but the choice would be a challenging one as the size, condition and geographic location had to be seriously weighed up. With operators still withdrawing steamers, it was hardly the best time to start operating one! The Neyland ferry *Alumchine* was the first paddle steamer to be considered for preservation and operation. This fine little paddle steamer was small and economic enough for the preservation group to run and negotiations were soon commenced to purchase her. Sadly, these came to nothing and the steamer was scrapped soon afterwards. The failure with the *Alumchine* meant that a new candidate for preservation was required.

**ABOVE** *Tattershall Castle* moored on the Thames Embankment at London in April 1976. This steamer found a new life on the Thames after she had been withdrawn from service on the Humber. *Tattershall Castle* has had a long career as a static paddle steamer and has outlived several others that have been burnt out or sold.
*Andrew Gladwell*

**ABOVE** With such an abundance of paddle steamers becoming available for purchase and preservation, the preservationists faced a difficult choice of what to do first. However, when the River Dart paddle steamer *Kingswear Castle* was withdrawn, she became the perfect candidate for preservation and was purchased by the PSPS. *Andrew Gladwell*

**BELOW** *Kingswear Castle* at the Medway Bridge Marina on the River Medway in 1973. The steamer had been on the Medway for only a short while at the time. She faced more than a decade of restoration work by dedicated volunteers before she was steamed again in November 1983, for the first time in many years. *PSPS Collection*

**ABOVE** *Waverley* became the subject of a major campaign during the early 1970s. The campaign was headed by the charismatic team of Douglas McGowan and Terry Sylvester. Eventually, she was offered to the PSPS for £1 in November 1973. *PSPS Collection*

**BELOW** *Waverley* on the Firth of Clyde during the early 1970s. At the time, her uniqueness was being promoted to try to ensure that she had an operational future. This included painting her vented paddle box black to emphasise her special place in the Clyde fleet. Exclusive cruises were also operated. *Andrew Gladwell*

*Waverley* departing from Dunoon in July 1971. When the PSPS was offered the *Waverley* it was the start of a massive project: her future was argued about and 1,001 challenges were faced but one easy decision was to return her funnels to the old LNER colours of red, black and white. *John Gilmore*

**LEFT** *Waverley* looked magnificent in her restored LNER funnel livery. Her acquisition meant that hard questions had to be asked as to whether to operate her or to preserve her in a static role. Thankfully, the decision was taken to operate her but this was hampered by the routes that she could serve. Her directors, officers and crew possessed great dedication over what were incredibly challenging early years. *Andrew Gladwell*

**RIGHT** *Waverley's* brand image was firmly promoted to her many fans who purchased a wide range of souvenirs from her shop, which included bobble hats, shopping bags, sweatshirts and china mugs. All bore her famous red, black and white colour scheme. *Andrew Gladwell Collection*

**BELOW RIGHT** *Waverley* gained a UK-wide base of fans after she entered her preservation career in 1975. Four of the fans are shown here. They had all paid to travel south with her as passengers when she undertook her first season away from the Firth of Clyde. *Andrew Gladwell*

**BELOW** *Waverley's* first trip away from her native Firth of Clyde was in 1977 when she visited Llandudno as part of its centenary celebrations. This invitation prompted a more ambitious programme during the following year with the highlight being a short season of cruises on the River Thames. *Andrew Gladwell*

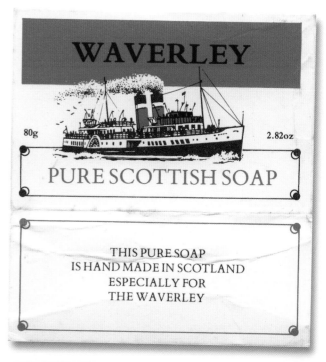

*Waverley* cruising on the Firth of Clyde during the mid-1970s. *Waverley* quickly settled into a timetable that involved her operating cruises from Glasgow as well as regular sailings from new places such as Ayr. Popular cruises included those to Arran and through the Kyles of Bute. *PSPS Collection*

**ABOVE** The 16 months after *Waverley* was purchased by the Paddle Steamer Preservation Society and before her first preservation sailing were the most hectic in her career. A great deal of activity and uncertainty marked the months before she sailed again in May 1975. *Andrew Gladwell*

**BELOW** *Kingswear Castle* on her steaming trials on the River Medway in November 1983. This heralded the end of a long restoration during the 1970s and 1980s by group of dedicated volunteers that painstakingly restored her to her pristine 1924 condition. She re-entered full passenger service again in 1985, having gained a licence to carry up to 235 passengers. *PSPS Collection*

ABOVE *Waverley* in the 1970s on the Firth of Clyde. Her preservation has meant that the last large Firth of Clyde paddle steamer survived for future generations to enjoy. *PSPS Collection*

BELOW *Kingswear Castle* alongside Tower Pier, London around 1985. The mid-1980s were the peak of pleasure steamer preservation in the UK when *Balmoral* and *Kingswear Castle* were newly restored and joined *Waverley* in providing cruises around the UK. *PSPS Collection*

ABOVE *Kingswear Castle* provided a programme of regular cruises on the Medway and Thames after her restoration. For many years she made regular trips to London and is seen here close to the former Billingsgate market. On occasions, she went up the river as far as Putney. *Andrew Gladwell*

FACING PAGE TOP *Prince Ivanhoe* was an excellent consort for the *Waverley* and had been acquired after service at Portsmouth. Her career was tragically cut short when she sank on the Bristol Channel in 1981. She is shown here at Ilfracombe on Royal Wedding day – 29 July 1981. *Andrew Gladwell*

FACING PAGE BOTTOM *Balmoral* at Ramsgate in September 1987. She entered her preservation career as consort to *Waverley* in 1986. Her role was to increase the usage of piers and therefore to make them more viable as well as to provide a back-up vessel if *Waverley* failed, which was what happened in 1987. That year *Balmoral* had shown the sense in acquiring her. *Andrew Gladwell*

## *Waverley, Balmoral* and *Kingswear Castle*

In 1965, the unstable future of the distinctive River Dart paddle steamer *Kingswear Castle* was recognised and the preservationists became eager to assist her operators to keep her in service. Despite having had money spent on her just a few years earlier, her withdrawal from the River Dart was announced. Happily, she was sold to the Paddle Steamer Preservation Society for £600. This modest sum was a gesture of the River Dart Steamboat Company's sentimentality towards its last operational paddle steamer. The preservationists had, by this point, gained experience in acquiring and preserving a paddle steamer and funds were also largely in place to make the project achievable. The *Kingswear Castle* offered considerable potential as its design was traditional and beautiful but although the steamer was purchased the enthusiasts did not at the time have the means to restore and operate her. It was soon found that it was easy to acquire a paddle steamer but the

**ABOVE** *Medway Queen* high and dry whilst at the River Medina on the Isle of Wight where she found a home after her withdrawal from service in 1963. The charter to the Ridett family was not a success and decades of uncertainty followed until she returned to the River Medway during the mid-1980s. *PSPS Collection*

**BELOW** Pleasure steamers face a vastly different world in the 21st century than they did when they were built. Tighter health and safety and lifesaving regulations has meant that steamers need to constantly upgrade and improve. A great deal of this has been made possible by grants from the Heritage Lottery Fund. *Andrew Gladwell*

A view from *Balmoral* sailing in the Menai Strait. North Wales provided some of the very best cruises in the UK with its picturesque villages and resorts and attractive waters such as the Menai Strait, all viewed from the finest platform - a pleasure steamer. *Balmoral* has operated for both P. & A. Campbell and Waverley Excursions in North Wales.
*Andrew Gladwell*

*Waverley* arriving at Rothesay in her heyday. She is now the last sea-going paddle steamer in the world and, along with *Kingswear Castle* and *Balmoral*, continues the UK pleasure steamer tradition.
*PSPS Collection*

of special charters to promote *Waverley's* 'uniqueness' and her importance to the tourism on the Firth of Clyde, and the steamer herself underwent several changes to her appearance to emphasise how she differed from the car ferries. The sheer energy and vision displayed by the team promoting *Waverley* was rewarded when in November 1973 she was surprisingly offered to the Paddle Steamer Preservation Society for the princely sum of £1.

The initial excitement and enthusiasm of handing over the pound note was almost instantly met with the reality of the number of challenges that had to be dealt with on a daily basis. It fell to a small but perfectly matched group of individuals to face the challenges head on. The future of *Waverley* was quickly debated during those initial months and various options were explored for both a static and operational future. Just about every challenge was directed at her new owners, but they bravely decided to operate her at a time when it was possibly the hardest time to run a pleasure steamer successfully. With such a huge challenge, the new directors had to work flat-out to achieve their goal; once they had started, there was no option but to carry on and to get the job done. They acquired new skills that ranged from publicity, plumbing, flag designing and creating souvenirs to operating busy restaurants and bars.

*Waverley* embarked upon her preservation career in May 1975 amidst a blaze of publicity. The restoration of the striking LNER colours to her funnels heralded a bright new future for cruising on the Firth of Clyde and although the immediate years that followed were characterised by a more than ample number of problems, *Waverley* survived all of these. By the late 1970s, *Waverley* was becoming a success and although her day-to-day life was often shaky, her popularity increased. *Waverley* had simply become something special that had to be saved.

This passion for steam and heritage that manifested itself from the 1970s onwards drove many people to get involved with voluntary heritage activities. *Waverley* benefited from this as her continued operation and preservation relied on the crucial input from volunteers. This was particularly important during the long winter months when an army of people were needed to paint,

real problems came with operating one. *Kingswear Castle* was initially towed to the Isle of Wight and placed alongside the *Medway Queen*. Vandalism and lack of regular maintenance resulted in a vote in the PSPS being taken as to whether to restore or dispose of her. A positive decision was made and the *Kingswear Castle* was towed to the Medway Bridge Marina on the River Medway in Kent in 1971 to undergo restoration. Attention then turned towards the Firth of Clyde.

By the late 1960s, the Firth of Clyde fleet of paddle steamers had shrunk dramatically. Such well-loved examples as the *Jeanie Deans* and *Caledonia* had been acquired for static or operational use elsewhere and the Firth of Clyde had suddenly become an area where the paddle steamer was facing extinction, being replaced by functional car ferries that provided holidaymakers with the flexibility that they craved. By the early 1970s, *Waverley* had suddenly become the last of the Clyde steamers and a well-organised and enthusiastic campaign was launched to raise public awareness of the paddle steamer on the scenic Firth of Clyde. This was headed by the charismatic and highly energetic team of Terry Sylvester and Douglas McGowan and a strong, imaginative and highly effective publicity campaign was launched. This was backed up by a number

scrape and varnish the steamer for summer service. Others found a role in marketing, catering or administration. Even those that just supported the steamer by cruising carried their distinctive *Waverley* shopping bags or wore a *Waverley* bobble hat to promote the ship. The effect of all this meant that *Waverley* had a huge emotional pull and her fan-base significantly increased.

The most important year in *Waverley's* life was 1977 when she sailed away from the Firth of Clyde for the first time. The Clyde season was relatively short and dwindling, and many realised that *Waverley's* long-term survival was always on a knife edge. An increase in revenue was thought to be possible from other areas of the UK before and after the traditional Clyde season of June to late August, and an invitation to take part in the centenary celebrations of Llandudno Pier in 1977 enabled the bold leap to be made. The crowds at Llandudno, Fleetwood and Liverpool were truly spectacular and *Waverley* magically rekindled an interest in pleasure steamers as countless thousands in the North West saw *Waverley's* magnificent red, black and white funnels arrive at each destination. *Waverley's* highly successful operation away from the Firth of Clyde in 1977 onwards meant that a new UK-wide fan base was built up. From 1978, the full potential of the whole coastline of the UK was imaginatively exploited with timetables that made use of the old calling points of pleasure steamers, along with several new ones. The emotional climax came when *Waverley* first visited London in 1978 and Tower Bridge raised its bascules for her. *Waverley's* success was earned because she only offered a limited number of cruises in each area each year, stopping at each major calling point and maximising each day's sailing with an imaginative and complex timetable.

The successful operation of *Waverley* meant that the increased fan base for paddle steamers and growing revenue gave the *Kingswear Castle* project a much needed boost. A small and enthusiastic band of volunteers slowly worked to restore 'KC' to steam. With the success of *Waverley* and increase in membership of the preservation group, funds were passed to *Kingswear Castle* to accelerate restoration.

*Kingswear Castle* was steamed for the first time in November 1983. Just a year later, in 1984, *Waverley* and *Kingswear Castle* steamed together on the River Medway for the 'Parade of Steam' for the first time. The coal-fired *Kingswear Castle* entered full service in 1985 and was based at the newly opened Chatham Historic Dockyard in Kent. With her modest crew requirements, she was able to provide a range of popular day cruises to the old haunts of the Eagle Steamers such as Southend, Gravesend, London and the Thames Estuary.

By the early 1980s it became apparent that there was a need for *Waverley* to have an operational consort because

**FACING PAGE TOP** *Caledonia* departing from Rothesay in 1967. The graceful sight of a paddle steamer sweeping away from a pier has attracted passengers for over 200 years. *PSPS Collection*

**FACING PAGE BOTTOM** Paddle steamers have always gained a loyal following from passengers eager to embrace a world of polished brass, the spray from the sea and lashings of fresh air. *PSPS Collection*

of her success around the UK. This would enable her to have a back-up if she broke down and would also mean that a greater number of calls were possible with a two-ship operation, as well as ensuring that piers would be better maintained through greater use. The search for a suitable steamer took a long time and included vessels such as the *Queen of the Channel*. Eventually, the *Shanklin* that had operated between Portsmouth and the Isle of Wight was chosen. A gloriously fit-for-purpose steamer, she was renamed *Prince Ivanhoe* but sadly sank soon after her introduction in 1981. A replacement for her was then required and *Balmoral* entered service in 1986. The wisdom of acquiring *Balmoral* was soon in evidence as she made her first visit to the South Coast and Thames in September 1987 to stand in for *Waverley* when the paddler was withdrawn for repairs.

The mid-1980s were also marked by the reappearance of an old favourite when the *Medway Queen* was returned to the River Medway. Although she was in a poor condition after years of neglect and uncertainty over ownership, she was returning home at a time when there was hope once again for pleasure steamers.

The success of the *Waverley*, *Balmoral* and *Kingswear Castle* was mirrored by an equally large amount of preservation failure. Projects to place former pleasure steamers in static use such as the *Caledonia*, *Lincoln Castle* and *Ryde* met with eventual failure, and many former well-loved pleasure steamers spent decades of slow decline awaiting their fate.

By the 1990s, *Waverley*, *Balmoral* and *Kingswear Castle* were operating a pattern of annual cruises that fully utilised the old routes of the past as well as opening up many new locations. All three pleasure steamers by this stage had had long operational careers and some degree of rebuilding was crucial to give them a long-term future as well as restoring them to their original appearance. Changes were also required to their passenger accommodation to provide facilities that reflected modern needs, and the work had to be undertaken in compliance with stringent new safety regulations. In 2003, *Waverley* completed a major two-phase Heritage Lottery Fund 'Heritage Rebuild' to enable her to remain in operation for many more years. *Balmoral*

and *Kingswear Castle* also received Heritage Lottery Fund grants to give them brighter futures. In December 2012, *Kingswear Castle* was towed from the River Medway to start a new life in Devon. Another chapter had opened in the ever-changing life of UK pleasure steamers.

The initial years of the 21st century saw *Waverley*, *Balmoral* and *Kingswear Castle* continuing the 200-year-old pleasure steamer tradition. They were now facing a fast-changing consumer world where the internet was facilitating the way that people accessed passenger information. Passengers could book online as well as arranging accommodation and travel needs without leaving their armchair. Handbills, brochures and posters of the past had now been overtaken by new internet-led methods of promoting pleasure steamer cruises. It was clear that a new and rapidly changing marketing environment was providing fresh opportunities for the paddle steamers but also that passengers of the future would want the latest facilities and had different needs to their parents and grandparents.

**Conclusion**

The paddle steamer was one of the most recognisable products of Victorian and Edwardian times. It was a form of popular travel that represented pleasure and which played a massive role in the development of the British seaside resort. Alongside this, paddle propulsion was used widely for transporting goods to market and passengers

**ABOVE** *Balmoral, Kingswear Castle* and *Waverley* are the last of the pleasure steamers and provide river and coastal cruises around the UK. They conjure up the atmosphere of a bygone age and keep alive a tradition that goes back two centuries. *Andrew Gladwell*

overseas as well as being used for working tugs and ferries in busy harbours and rivers.

Paddle steamers were distinctive-looking vessels and possessed significant character. Fleets evolved with unique identities to create a loyal following amongst passengers. Steamers almost always had an attractive name associated with the area in which they operated, often taking the name of a well-known place or historical figure. Ornate and gilded carvings on the paddle boxes and bow made a strong visual statement about the steamer and its role. The stylish decoration gave the paddle steamer a certain grace and dignified appearance as it moved through the water. Each pleasure steamer had a distinct atmosphere and passengers became fiercely loyal to vessels such as *Embassy, Royal Daffodil, Balmoral, Jeanie Deans* or *Bristol Queen*, many returning year after year to see familiar officers and crew. Steamers became the 'poor man's liner' and enabled most people to experience the exhilarating atmosphere of travelling by sea to another place. They conveyed passengers in stylish accommodation, smoothly and quietly, the operation accompanied by the gentle hiss of the foamy wake from the paddle wheels. A trip on a

paddle steamer was, weather permitting, an exciting but ultimately relaxing experience.

The pleasure steamer in the 21st century has evolved to a point where the few remaining operational examples are cherished and their futures are assured due to their distinctiveness. People are attracted to them for many different reasons. For many of the older passengers, it is the heritage of these steamers that interest them as they look back nostalgically to the era when well-loved operating companies of yesteryear such as the Eagle Steamers and the Caledonian Steam Packet Company were operating. For younger generations and family groups, a cruise on a pleasure steamer is viewed as a tourist attraction and a new experience. But for most folk, pleasure steamers enable them to escape from everyday life and to enjoy the sensory and invigorating pleasures of sea breezes, fluttering flags, polished brass and the ever-changing coastal scenery that is unique to travel on water. All of these, combined with the glory of the UK coastline, make a cruise on a pleasure steamer as special now as it was for folk over a century ago.

**ABOVE** Famous and well-loved paddle steamers such as the *Caledonia* have now disappeared from the coastline of the UK. During their heyday, they became a popular and attractive part of the British seaside. *PSPS Collection*

**OVERLEAF** *Waverley* departing from Gravesend's Town Pier for London in October 2012. By this time, *Waverley* had gained worldwide fame and her importance to UK maritime heritage was recognised by her being included in the core collection of ships of national importance. *Andrew Gladwell*

Paddle steamers have faced changing fortunes as competition increased and other forms of transportation have evolved. Periods of prosperity were always matched with periods of decline but for over two centuries, pleasure steamers have adapted to changes in taste and needs. Britain, being an island, has a long, dramatic and ever-changing coastline and the very best way of admiring and discovering our rivers, coast and estuaries is aboard a steamer that was built purely for giving pleasure.

## Bibliography

Adams, Keith, *Red Funnel*, Richard Danielson, 2010

Adams, R. B., *Red Funnel and Before*, Kingfisher, 1986

Body, G., *British Paddle Steamers*, David and Charles, 1971

Burtt, Frank, *Steamers of the Thames and Medway*, Roadmaster Publishing, 1949

Clammer, Richard, *Cosens of Weymouth 1848-1918*, Black Dwarf Publications, 2005

Clammer, Richard, *Cosens of Weymouth 1918-1996*, Twelveheads Press, 2001

Clammer, Richard, *Kingswear Castle & the Paddle Steamers of the River Dart*, Twelveheads Press, 2013

Clammer, Richard, *Paddle Steamers*, Batsford, 1983

Collard, Chris, *P. & A. Campbell Pleasure Steamers 1887-1945*, Tempus, 1999

Collard, Chris, *P. & A Campbell Pleasure Steamers from 1946*, Tempus, 1999

Coombes, Nigel, *Passenger Steamers of the Bristol Channel – A Pictorial Record*, Twelveheads, 1990

Cox, Bernard, *Paddling Across the Bay*, Paddle Steamer Preservation Society, 1981

Cox, Bernard, *Pleasure Steamers*, David and Charles, 1983

Davies, Ken, *Solent Passages & Their Steamers*, Isle of Wight County Press, 1982

Duckworth, C., & Langmuir, Graham, *Clyde River & Other Steamers*, Brown, Son & Ferguson 1972

Duckworth, C., & Langmuir, Graham, *West Coast Steamers*, T. Stephenson & Sons Ltd, 1953

Dumpleton, Bernard, *The Story of the Paddle Steamer*, Venton Publications, 1973

Farr, Graham, *West Country Passenger Steamers*, T. Stephenson & Sons, 1967

Gladwell, Andrew, *Lancashire Coast Pleasure Steamers*, History Press, 2003

Gladwell, Andrew, *North Wales Pleasure Steamers*, Amberley, 2011

Gladwell, Andrew, *River Medway Pleasure Steamers*, Amberley, 2010

Hancock, H. E., *Semper Fidelis – The Story of the Navvies*, General Steam Navigation Co, 1949

Kittridge, Alan, *Passenger Steamers of the River Tamar*, Twelveheads, 1987

McCrorie, Ian, *Clyde Pleasure Steamers – An Illustrated History*, Orr, Pollock & Co, 1986

O'Brien, F. T., *Early Solent Steamers*, David and Charles, 1973

Plummer, Russell, *Paddle Steamers at War 1939-1945*, GMS Enterprises, 1995

Plummer, Russell, *Paddle Steamers in the 70s*, Anglia County Press, 1975

Thomas, John, *British Railway Steamers of the Clyde*, Ian Allan, 1948

Thompson, A. G., *The Thames – And All That, 1824-1935*, General Steam Navigation Co, 1935

Thornton, Edward, *South Coast Pleasure Steamers*, T. Stephenson & Sons, 1969

Wall, Robert, *Bristol Channel Pleasure Steamers*, David and Charles, 1973

Williams, David L., *Glory Days: Paddle Steamers*, Ian Allan, 2002

## Websites

www.heritagesteamers.co.uk – The Paddle Steamer Preservation Society Collection

www.waverleyexcursions.co.uk – Cruises by the paddle steamer *Waverley*

www.mvbalmoral.org.uk – Cruises by the vintage excursion steamer *Balmoral*

www.paddlesteamers.org.uk – The website of the Paddle Steamer Preservation Society

www.medwayqueen.co.uk – The 'Heroine of Dunkirk', the *Medway Queen*

www.dartmouthrailriver.co.uk – Paddle Steamer *Kingswear Castle* on the River Dart

## Acknowledgements

I would like to thank the following persons and organisations for their help in the preparation of this book:

Paddle Steamer Preservation Society
World Ship Society
Roy Asher
Alison Bradley
Jill Harvey
Chris Jones
Eric Jones
Ron Jones
Kieran McCarthy
John Richardson
Jean Spells
Waverley Excursions